HERBS
AND SPICES

by JULIA F. MORTON

Illustrated by
JEAN DAY ZALLINGER

 GOLDEN PRESS • NEW YORK
Western Publishing Company, Inc.
Racine, Wisconsin

FOREWORD

This guide presents 372 species of flavoring plants, both wild and cultivated. Beyond the classic favorites of medieval Europe and England, familiar in gardens of America, the book reveals the little-known savory products that give Mexican, Indonesian, and other regional dishes their distinctive character and zest. Included, too, are the ingredients that enhance many well-known manufactured or processed foods and beverages.

Jean Zallinger, the artist, has meticulously shown not only the identifying features of the plants but also the special parts used for seasoning.

Grateful acknowledgment is made to Dr. Richard A. Howard, Director, Arnold Arboretum, Harvard University; the New York Botanical Garden; the Royal Botanic Gardens, Kew, England; Dr. Brian Lawrence of Stange Canada Ltd. for generous cooperation in providing materials for the illustrator; and the USDA Subtropical Horticulture Research Station and others who furnished fresh or preserved specimens. The author is indebted especially to the Royal Botanic Gardens, to the Munich Botanical Garden, the botanical gardens of the University of Vienna, Michigan State University, and Charles Towne Landing, South Carolina, for the privilege of photographing plants in their charming herb plots. The unique resources of the Morton Collectanea, University of Miami, were indispensable in the selection of topics and in the preparation of the text.   J. F. M.

CONTENTS

A NOTE ON GEOGRAPHICAL NAMES

Many traditional place names have been retained here because they abound in the historical and botanical literature on herbs and spices. Some examples of place names recently changed are Madagascar (now the Malagasy Republic) and Ceylon (now Sri Lanka).

HERBS AND SPICES

From earliest times herbs and spices have been prized both as preservatives and as masks for meat, fish, and other foods past their prime. Equally important, they have satisfied man's natural craving for flavor—that remarkable blend of aroma and taste. Even today, primitive people in many areas of the world nibble on leaves, roots, stems, or other plant parts for flavor enjoyment and to relieve thirst. Modern outdoorsmen—campers, hunters, foresters, biological field workers, and explorers—turn to tart or pungent wild plants for the same reasons.

In the kitchen, herbs and spices, with their enticing piquant or aromatic qualities, serve mainly to enhance the flavor of food, whether in everyday cooking or gourmet dishes. Today more people than ever before have the opportunity to eat for pleasure rather than solely to satisfy hunger. The food industry, responding to the increasingly sophisticated palates of consumers, employs a vast array of flavorings to make products more appetizing. People on low-sodium diets learn to make dishes so savory with herbs and spices that the lack of salt goes unnoticed. Even toothpastes, mouthwashes, and other toiletries are given an appealing taste and aroma through the use of herbs and spices.

Scientists have discovered that man experiences just four basic tastes, each noticed at a different spot on the tongue: sweet, at the tip; salt, on either side of the tip; sour, further back on both sides; and bitter, in the center at the rear. Preferences may vary with age and culture, but the great diversity of aromatic plants available enables us to readily satisfy our desire for any favorite taste sensation.

Culinary and healing herbs in the Chelsea Physic (meaning "natural") Garden, London, created in 1763.

HERBS (pp. 11-93). The distinction between herbs and spices has been variously defined. In this book herbs are truly herbaceous (nonwoody) plants or semiwoody subshrubs. Exceptions are the rose, sweet gale, and rosemary, which with age become woody shrubs but are grown in herb gardens as annuals.

The plants described all qualify as flavoring herbs: their leaves, stems, flowers, or roots (and sometimes seeds) are used for seasoning, or their leaves are steeped for tea. Not included are strictly medicinal or poisonous herbs, those eaten mainly as vegetables, and those grown only for fragrance or ornamental value. Most species described are suitable for cultivation both in home gardens and commercial plantations. For that reason brief notes are given on means of propagation and on cultural requirements.

SPICES (pp. 94-155) described in this book fall into four categories: (1) aromatic lichens; (2) any part of a tree or woody shrub or vine used for flavoring; (3) roots, flowers, seeds, or fruits of herbaceous plants such as saffron and ginger, the leaves of which are not used for flavoring; and (4) extracts or essential oils of any of these plants.

Not covered here are plants such as safflower (Carthamus tinctorius) and annatto (Bixa orellana) and alkanet (Alkanna tinctoria). Although often associated with spices, these plants provide color only and actually have no true "spice," or flavoring, function.

Unlike herbs, spices, with few exceptions, are not easily grown in home gardens, but are usually available only as products that are processed and distributed commercially.

Window boxes, hanging baskets, and clay pots are admirably suited for growing kitchen herbs on a small scale, allowing even the apartment-dweller to enjoy fresh seasonings. Outdoors, a wide variety of herbs can be grown in simple rectangular beds; low, slow-growing species are ideal for informal rock gardens.

Medieval herb gardens, designed to please the eye as well as the palate, were laid out in intricate patterns. Your garden, too, can be as imaginative in design as inclination and space allow. If a special plot is not feasible, herbs may serve as edgings along paths or as borders around flower beds. Beds raised from 1-3 ft. high are often the most practical where nematodes are troublesome, and the higher levels eliminate the need for stooping when gardening. Such raised beds often serve as sections of a garden wall.

Mulches (organic, paper, or black polyethylene) reduce the labor of weeding. Sterilized soil is best and it should not be so rich as to promote rapid growth. Herbs planted in poor, fairly dry soil are easier to control and richer in aromatic properties.

Most of the literature on herbs and herb growing includes many species that are solely ornamental, medicinal, or fragrant, for in the past the importance of herb gardens as sources of medicines and perfumes equaled their role as suppliers of culinary seasonings. Today, however, we can rely on the druggist for our medicinal and cosmetic needs and, choosing from the wide range of species presented here, concentrate efforts on strictly culinary herbs.

Among the factors the herb gardener should consider in selecting species are: (1) whether the plants are

The Knot Garden, an intricate herb plot at the Brooklyn Botanic Garden in New York.

annual, biennial, or perennial; (2) their climatic requirements; (3) preference for sun or shade; (4) size of mature plant; (5) rate of growth; (6) ability to tolerate pruning; and (7) appearance before and after flowering or fruiting. Taller plants should be placed in the rear or center of the bed; low-growing species should be reserved for edgings and borders.

Most herbs familiar in the United States are of European origin, and traditional herb gardening is based on practices and plants suited to temperate and sub-temperate climates where seeds are sown in flats indoors during the winter and the seedlings transplanted to the garden in the spring. Because books on subtropical and tropical gardening seldom discuss herb growing, the impression prevails that prospects for herb gardening are limited in those regions. This book should dispel that belief, as it provides a universal view of natural flavoring materials.

For use fresh, pick the tender tips and young leaves of herbs as needed. Most herbs will continue to supply new foliage even if cut back several times during the growing season.

For preservation, most herbs should be harvested just as they begin to bloom; at that time their essential oil content is at a peak. However, plants of the mint family are most aromatic when in full bloom. Harvest young leafy tips, individual leaves, flowering tops, or flowers early in the morning on a dry, sunny day, just as the dew is disappearing. If herbs are picked later in the day, too much of the essential oil will have been dissipated by the sun. For cutting for bunches, be sure to allow sufficient stem length.

European cooks have traditionally preserved herbs between layers of salt in stone crocks, or by immersion in pure olive oil. More common methods of preservation today are air-drying and quick-freezing.

For air-drying, remove defective leaves and any tough stems, rinse the herbs, shake off excess water, and drain them on absorbent towels. Do not dry herbs in the sun, as they will lose both aromatic quality and color. It is best to dry them in a shady, dry, dust-free atmosphere, preferably indoors where they are protected from dew and rain. An air-conditioned room is ideal, but any well-ventilated room will suffice. Oven drying removes much essential oil, but is necessary in wet weather and for drying chives, which turn yellow and lose flavor if dried by any slower method.

Hang bunches of herbs near the ceiling, in nylon-mesh bags. Or spread the herbs on wire mesh trays that have been suspended or elevated so air can circulate on all sides. Thoroughly dried herbs will rustle when stirred or shaken. They can be stored whole, ground, or pulverized in air-tight, opaque jars or in tins, in a cool, dry location.

Flowers and herbs for sachets or potpourri are usually air-dried. They retain more color if layered with borax, cornstarch, or flour and stored in uncovered boxes for about two weeks.

For freezing, tie rinsed herbs in small bunches and plunge them immediately into boiling water for one minute; then immerse them in ice water for two minutes. After thorough draining, seal them in plastic bags, label, and pack the bags loosely in frozen-food boxes in the freezer.

SEEDS for replanting or for seasoning should be harvested when the pods have turned brown but before they have split open fully. To avoid loss of seeds, hold a container under the pods while clipping them from the dry stems. Dry the pods in the sun for a few days, taking them indoors at night and during showers. When dry, rub the pods between your hands or crush them lightly to release the seeds. Separate the seeds from the pods and store them in transparent labeled jars.

ROOTS AND SMALL BULBS should be sun-dried. Turn them daily to assure uniform dehydration. As an extra precaution, place them in a barely warm oven, leaving the door open for a brief time. Slice thick roots crosswise or lengthwise before drying.

A mid-19th-century American spice box (courtesy George W. Rosner, Univ. Miami Library) made of bronze-painted tin. It holds five canisters for spices and a cylindrical nutmeg grater.

CULINARY USES

The creative cook knows that the addition of fresh or dried herbs to ordinary dishes makes any meal more interesting and satisfying.

Fresh herbs are used primarily as garnishes for all kinds of foods and soft drinks, and as ingredients in salads, sandwiches, soups, and stews. Herbs are chopped and sprinkled on cooked vegetables, eggs, seafood, and cheese dishes, and blended into sauces.

Dried herbs are most often used to season meats, dressings and stuffings, and pickles. Flowers and fresh roots may be candied or crystallized, or preserved in syrup or spiced vinegar. Fresh or dried herbs are steeped for tea, called tisane.

The most common culinary uses are included with the descriptions of herbs in this book.

A NOTE OF CAUTION

The small amounts of herbs and spices used to give added zest to foods can usually be ingested without fear of adverse effects. However, active principles occurring in many herbs and spices, such as oxalates (in sorrel) or tannins (in myrtle), make them unfit for consumption in large quantities. In some cases, toxic components, such as safrole (in sassafras and massoia bark), thujone (in tansy and wormwood), and cocaine (in coca), are removed to make the plant product safe for commercial use in foods or beverages.

The consumer's best protection is to keep well informed. For this reason, the presence of known harmful constituents is mentioned in this book where it seems advisable.

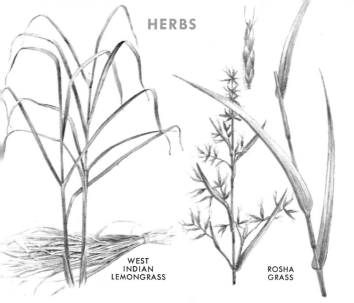

WEST
INDIAN
LEMONGRASS

ROSHA
GRASS

GRAMINEAE (Grass Family)

WEST INDIAN LEMONGRASS (*Cymbopogon citratus*), of unknown origin, is cultivated in all tropical and subtropical climates and sometimes in greenhouses. It is a perennial, growing in tufts, with erect, delightfully lemon-scented leaves (3-5 ft. long, ½ in. wide). Flower stalk (to 2 ft.) is rarely seen. In the home kitchen, the leaf bases and stems are used raw as food seasoning and as flavoring for wines, liquors, and soft drinks; the leaf blade is used to flavor fish, soups, curries, pickles, and sauces. Leaf infusion is drunk hot or cold as a pleasant tea.

EAST INDIAN LEMONGRASS (*C. flexuosus*) is native and cultivated in India. It yields lemongrass oil, used by food manufacturers in beverages, ice cream, candy, baked goods, gelatin desserts, and chewing gum, and valued in cosmetic and pharmaceutical products. *C. martini*, called **ROSHA GRASS,** or **GERANIUM GRASS,** is the source of palmarosa oil used mainly for perfumery. The oil from **CITRONELLA** (*C. nardus*) is used for flavoring and in scenting soap and is widely known as an insect repellent. All species are propagated by root division.

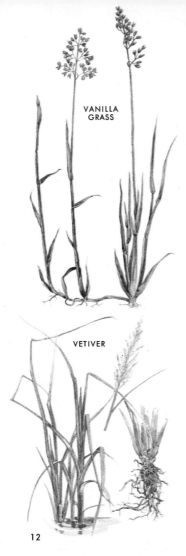

VANILLA GRASS

VETIVER

VANILLA GRASS (*Hierochloe odorata*), also called **SWEET GRASS, SENECA GRASS, HOLY GRASS**, and, in Poland, **ZU-BROVKA**, is native to moist places from Russia and Bulgaria west to the British Isles and in North America as far south as New Jersey and Arizona. The flat, erect leaves (1-2 ft. high, to ¼ in. wide) have a strong vanilla fragrance lasting indefinitely. In Poland, one or more blades are put in a bottle of vodka for flavoring, and small packets of the grass are sold in the United States for this purpose. Essential oil is esteemed in France for flavoring candy, soft drinks, and tobacco. It is much used in perfume blending. Vanilla grass is a favorite material for weaving baskets; it was formerly strewn before the doors of European churches. Dried, it has been burned as incense; also used in pillows and to scent clothing. Propagated by division.

VETIVER, or **KHUS-KHUS** (*Vetiveria zizanioides*), of India, Burma, and Ceylon, and much grown throughout the tropics, is a coarse, clumped grass (to 5 ft.) with scentless leaves and fibrous, spongy, aromatic roots. Essential oil from the roots is used in India to season fruit drinks. In vegetable-canning, it is added to enhance the flavor of asparagus. Vetiver is highly valued in perfumes. Fresh roots, interwoven and kept wet, are hung as screens in Oriental windows and doorways; dried roots are made into fans and also serve to scent and protect clothing from insects.

ARACEAE (Arum Family)

SWEET FLAG (*Acorus calamus*) is a perennial herb of freshwater marshes in temperate climates; often planted in moist areas of gardens. The aromatic, erect sword-shaped leaves (2-6 ft.) rise from a horizontal rootstock (to 1 in. thick). Fragrant, pungent sweet flag has been used in medicine, perfume, snuff, insecticides, and flavoring. Fresh or dried, it has been candied, used as a substitute for ginger, or added to home-brew or wine. The leaves were formerly strewn on church floors. Commercially, the rootstock, or calamus oil derived from it, has been used in soft drinks, ice cream, baked goods, vinegar, bitters, vermouth, gin, Benedictine, and brandies. Recent evidence of toxicity is curtailing use in foods and beverages. The ornamental variety *variegatus* has vertical yellow stripes. Propagated by division.

GRASS-LEAVED SWEET FLAG (*Acorus gramineus*) occurs wild along valley streams in Japan and is common in Southeast Asia and the East Indies. The leaves (to 1/6 in. wide and to 1 ft. long) stand in dense tufts. The rootstock is stronger and pleasanter in odor and flavor than that of *A. calamus* and is similarly used, but especially in medical preparations. A variety with white-striped leaves is often planted near pools and in hanging baskets. Dwarf variety *pusillus* is only 2-3 in. high. Propagated by division.

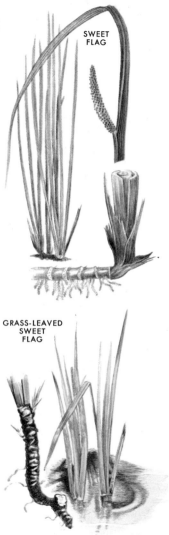

SWEET FLAG

GRASS-LEAVED SWEET FLAG

13

AMARYLLIDACEAE (Amaryllis Family)

SHALLOT (*Allium ascalonicum*) is believed indigenous to Asia Minor and is less hardy than the onion. It is cultivated more commonly in England, Europe, Africa, and Asia than in the United States, where the name shallot is applied to a small red onion. Leaves slender, cylindrical; the pear-shaped bulb splits into bulblets ("cloves"). The outer skin is gray at the top and red below; the inner, violet at the top and greenish below. Bulblets are minced to flavor soups, stews, and meats and are also pickled. The flavor is milder than that of garlic. Young leaves are eaten in salads. The dried bulbs keep well for a year. Grown as an annual, mainly from bulbs since seedlings vary. Harvested when the leaves die.

LEEK (*Allium porrum*) may be a variety known only in cultivation of *A. ampeloprasum*; grows wild from Scotland to North Africa. Of classical fame, it was favored by Nero and is the emblem of Wales. Rare in United States; popular in Europe, Central America, and East Indies. Varieties such as American Flag tolerate low elevations in tropics. Plant is biennial; may reach 4½ ft. with neck 20 in. long and 4 in. thick, the indistinct bulb slightly broader. Strong in odor but mild in taste, leaves and neck used mainly to flavor soups (notably vichyssoise) and salads. Entire plant may be cooked as a vegetable. "Perpetual" types grown from offshoots but most from seed. Heads are cut in fall, dried until spring.

SHALLOT

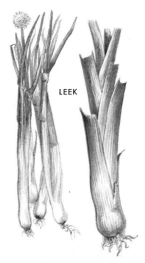

LEEK

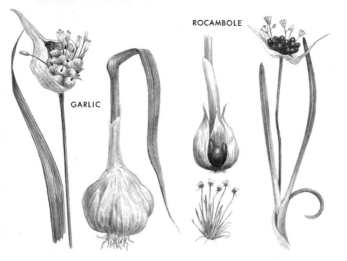

ROCAMBOLE

GARLIC

GARLIC (*Allium sativum*), native to central Asia and most prized in Latin countries, grows easily in both cool and warm climates. It is a perennial herb with flat leaves (to 1 ft. long and 1 in. wide) and a silky-skinned bulb composed of 4 to 15 bulblets, or "cloves." Though eaten with bread by some, garlic is mainly a potent seasoning. A clove may be merely rubbed in the salad bowl; or minced garlic, garlic juice, dehydrated powder, or distilled oil employed to give zest to soups, sauces, dressings, meats, fowl, fish, pickles, curries, and chutneys. Seeds, leaves, and stems are sometimes used as well. The cloves are planted; the plants pulled up in 5 or 6 months, dried for a week, and then trimmed or braided and hung in the shade to dry.

ROCAMBOLE (*Allium scorodoprasum*), also called **SAND LEEK**, occurs wild from Scandinavia to Syria. It is a hardy perennial with flat, hairy-edged leaves (6-8 in. long, ⅜-⅝ in. wide). The flower stalk is twisted at the top and most or all of the flowers develop into bulbils. Seeds are rarely formed. The compound underground bulb produces several stalked offsets. The "cloves" are generally smaller than those of garlic and milder in flavor but are used similarly. Tender new leaves are eaten in salads. Both aerial and underground bulbs are divided for planting. Variety *minus*, known as **LESSER-LEAVED GARLIC**, is slender with narrow, brown-skinned bulbs. Rocambole is often utilized in French-Canadian cookery.

CHIVES

GARLIC CHIVES

CHIVES (*Allium schoenoprasum*), indigenous to Europe and much of Asia, is a fast-growing perennial widely cultivated in cool and warm climates. Slim, hollow leaves (to 2 ft. or more) rise in thick tufts from slender, white-sheathed bulbs which develop in dense masses. The leaves are cut off close to the ground for use and are soon replaced by new growth—3 to 4 times before dormancy where there are cold winters. Tender and mild, the fresh, chopped leaves are popular additions to salad dressings, sauces, cheeses, omelets, soups, croquettes, and sausages, and as garnish on mashed potatoes, green salads, and sliced tomatoes. The bulbs are often pickled. Propagated by division or, less commonly, from seeds, the flower stalk being generally eliminated. Beds may be replanted every 3 or 4 years. Easily grown indoors in flowerpots.

GARLIC CHIVES (*Allium tuberosum*), otherwise known as **CHINESE CHIVES** or **ORIENTAL GARLIC**, is native and cultivated in subtropical China, India, and the East Indies. It is an attractive perennial, growing in clumps 6 to 10 in. high. The 2 to 3 leaves (1/4 in. wide) are flat, solid, and dark green. Instead of a single bulb, 1 to 3 tubers develop on a horizontal rootstock. The tender tops, rich in calcium, phosphorus, and iron, and mildly garliclike in odor and flavor, are chopped and added to salads and cottage cheese, or put in soup just prior to serving. Cooking destroys the flavor.

IRIDACEAE (Iris Family)

ORRIS ROOT is derived from the German iris (*Iris germanica*), the fleur-de-lis (*I. germanica* var. *florentina*), and the sweet iris (*I. pallida*). All are European, grown as ornamentals in temperate regions and commercially in Italy, Morocco, Iran, and India. They are perennial herbs (2-3 ft. high) with erect, flat leaves (¾-2 in. wide), fragrant flowers, and rhizomes (¾-1¼ in. thick) which are nearly odorless when fresh. Peeled, and dried for several months, they develop the violetlike fragrance prized in perfumes, cosmetics, soaps, and dentifrices. Orris oil, mainly from *I. pallida*, is used to flavor soft drinks, candies, and chewing gum, and to enhance fruit flavors in food manufacturing.

SWEET IRIS

ORRIS ROOT

GERMAN IRIS

PIPERACEAE (Pepper Family)

MAKULAN (*Piper auritum*) is native and common in moist areas at low elevations from southern Mexico to Colombia. An herb, usually to 6 ft., sometimes semi-woody and up to 20 ft., it has thin, soft leaves (to 2 ft. long, 15 in. wide) and minute flowers and seeds borne in spikes (⅛ in. thick, to 10 in. long). Leaves have a strong, sarsaparillalike aroma, are much used in Mexico to season tamales, in Guatemala for flavoring many foods, particularly meat dishes and freshwater snails. In Honduras, young leaves are sometimes cooked and eaten as greens.

MAKULAN

MYRICACEAE (Sweet Gale Family)

SWEET GALE (*Myrica gale*), also called **BOG MYRTLE** and **MEADOW FERN**, occurs wild across the Northern Hemisphere. It is a deciduous shrub (2-5 ft. high); the leaves are glossy above, pale and downy beneath. Male flowers in ½ in. catkins; fruiting spikes massed with tiny yellowish nutlets. Wood, leaves, and fruits resinously aromatic. Leaves often used to season soups and meats, and are dried for tea. In England, leaves and branches serve to flavor ale, thus known as gale beer. Nutlets are also used as spice. Sweet gale bark is a source of dye, and the boiled catkins yield wax used for making fragrant candles.

SWEET
GALE

SORREL

POLYGONACEAE (Buckwheat Family)

SORREL (*Rumex acetosa*) grows wild and in gardens from temperate Asia through Europe and North America and is cultivated in Africa. It is a perennial herb (to 3½ ft.) with alternate, variable leaves (3-5 in. long), which turn red with age. Acid in flavor, the young leaves were very popular with early Egyptians and Romans and have been much used in soups, salads, and omelets, in sauces for lamb, veal, pork, duck, and goose, and by the Laplanders in reindeer-milk whey. Because of their oxalate content, they should be eaten sparingly; for use as greens they should be boiled in 2 or 3 waters. Grown from seeds—which are used in Sweden to make bread—and also by root-division. Spreads rapidly and is likely to become a weed.

FRENCH SORREL (*Rumex scutatus*), native to central and southern Europe, North Africa, and western Asia, and cultivated in mild-temperate climates, is a perennial herb (to 2 ft. high) with slender, reclining or erect stems and gray-green, slightly fleshy leaves (to 1½ in. long), rounded or heart-shaped, with narrow protrusions at the base. Exceedingly acid, French sorrel is used solely as a flavoring. The leaves give zest to less flavorful greens in salads, are also used in sauces and in the much-esteemed French sorrel soup. Despite its reputation as a digestive aid, the plant is definitely unwholesome in quantity. Flowering tops are often dried for decorative purposes. Propagated by seeds or division, drought-tolerant.

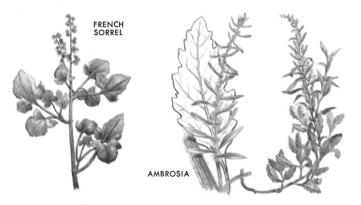

FRENCH
SORREL

AMBROSIA

CHENOPODIACEAE (Goosefoot Family)

AMBROSIA (*Chenopodium ambrosioides*), also called **MEXICAN TEA** (**EPAZOTE** in Mexico), is indigenous to Mexico but widely naturalized and cultivated in most warm countries. It is an annual or perennial herb, erect (to 3½ ft.), many-branched, with soft downy leaves (to 3½ in. long). Entire plant is strongly aromatic and used for food flavoring by the Maya Indians of Yucatan. The leaves are highly esteemed in Mexico and Guatemala for seasoning corn, black beans, mushrooms, fish, and shellfish. Leaf infusion is a popular herb tea in Mexico, southern France, Germany, and the West Indies. The plant is widely used as a folk remedy for intestinal parasites; oil of chenopodium is no longer so used in the United States.

19

CARYOPHYLLACEAE (Pink Family)

CARNATION, or **CLOVE PINK** (*Dianthus caryophyllus*), is a perennial herb, wild from western France to India. While many large types of various colors are bred for the florist trade, those raised for herb gardens are the richly scented, deep-red clove carnations or the Perpetual Border varieties. Petals with bitter white heel snipped off are steeped in hot water and sugar and boiled down to syrup. They are also added to white vinegar, which is left in the sun for a few days, or are pickled in vinegar with cinnamon and mace and then mashed to make sauce for lamb. The petals are candied by coating with beaten egg whites and powdered sugar. The dwarf **SPICE PINK** (*D. graniticus*), with purplish flowers, is grown for fragrance.

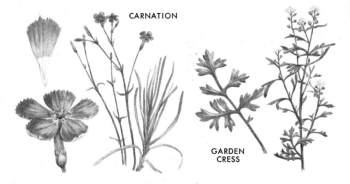

CARNATION

GARDEN CRESS

CRUCIFERAE (Mustard Family)

GARDEN CRESS (*Lepidium sativum*), wild in western Asia and cultivated in all temperate climates, is a fast-growing annual herb (6 in.-2 ft. high), with a single erect stem and leaves (to 2 in. long) more or less lobed or finely cut, crisped, and curled. **GOLDEN CRESS** is a dwarf variety with scalloped, yellow-green foliage. The young leaves are pungent in flavor, and have a long history of use as a garnish for meats and in salads and curries. They must be cut before the plant blooms, else they are tough and acrid. Planting some seeds every 8 or 14 days yields a continual supply, with a new crop ready for cutting in 4 to 6 weeks. The seeds are minute (14,000 to the ounce) and remain viable for 5 years. They are much used medicinally in Asia.

WATERCRESS (*Nasturtium officinale*) occurs wild in shallow, moving fresh water from western Asia to southern Sweden and Scotland and it has become naturalized in temperate and milder regions around the world. It is an evergreen, fast-growing, perennial herb, rooting in stream beds, extending (2-4 ft.) to the surface and floating. Pungent young shoots are cut once a week for use as a garnish, or in salads, sandwiches, omelets, soup, and dressings, or steamed with rice. If purity of the water source is in doubt, the shoots should be dipped in a weak solution of iodine, potassium permanganate, or other suitable disinfectant. Propagated by cuttings or roots. Multiplies by spreading roots and self-sowing of seeds. May be grown in gardens or greenhouses with ample irrigation and added lime.

HORSERADISH (*Armoracia lapathifolia*), native to southeastern Europe, is naturalized and cultivated in the British Isles and northeastern United States. It is a long-lived perennial herb with rippled leaves (to 15 in. long and to 9 in. wide) and a woody root (6-12 in. long, 1-2 in. thick) of pungent, mustardlike odor and hot, stinging taste prized by the ancient Greeks. The young leaves are added to salads. The root, grated or ground and blended with vinegar (sometimes also egg yolk or heavy cream) and combined with a little salt, sugar, or mustard, is often served as a condiment with oysters or boiled beef. Fresh root or dehydrated flakes used in other sauces, relishes, dressings, and soups. Grown from root cuttings. The related **WASABI** (*Eutrema wasabi*) of Japan has a similar root used in the same way.

WATERCRESS

HORSERADISH

ROSACEAE (Rose Family)

ROSES (species of *Rosa*), while not herbaceous plants, are time-honored members of the herb garden. Favored for potpourri and culinary use are: the European **DOG ROSE** (*R. canina*), with flowers typically white to deep-pink; the **EGLANTINE**, or **SWEET BRIER** (*R. eglanteria*), with small, bright pink flowers; the **FRENCH ROSE** (*R. gallica*), pink to crimson, of which variety *officinalis*, the "Apothecary's Rose," has been much used in herbal medicine; the **CABBAGE**, or **PROVENCE ROSE** (*R. centifolia*), from the eastern Caucasus, with fragrant, double, pink flowers; the **DAMASK ROSE** (*R. damascena*), from Asia Minor, with large scented flowers, white to red; and the **RAMANAS ROSE** (*R. rugosa*) of northern China, Korea, and Japan, with fragrant red or white blossoms and leaves that turn golden in the fall. A hybrid between the dog and damask (*R. X alba* var. *suaveolens*) is an important source of attar of roses, an essential oil from the petals. Rose petals are often used fresh as garnishes on salads and fruit cups and under the crust of cherry pies before baking. Rose buds may be pickled in white

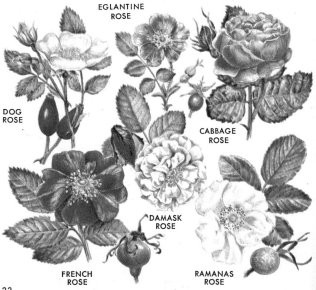

EGLANTINE ROSE

DOG ROSE

CABBAGE ROSE

DAMASK ROSE

FRENCH ROSE

RAMANAS ROSE

vinegar and sugar, or ground up with sugar to make a conserve which lasts indefinitely if stirred daily for three months and kept tightly sealed. A cooked preserve or jam is made by soaking, draining, and then boiling rose petals with sugar and lemon juice, adding the drained-off liquid gradually. A popular confection of the Near East is made of rose petals and honey. Petals are also steeped in vinegar to impart a rose flavor, and are often crystallized or made into syrup or lozenges. Dried petals give bouquet and flavor to tea and tisanes. In the food industry, attar of roses, rose absolute and, to a lesser extent, rose water, are used in flavoring beverages, candy, ice cream, bakery goods, gelatin desserts, and jelly. The fruits of roses, called **ROSE HIPS**, are eaten raw, and are also used in jellies, sauces, tarts, wines, and distilled liqueurs. They are much used in vitamin preparations in the natural "health food" trade, as they are rich in ascorbic acid. Hips of the **BURNET ROSE** (*R. spinosissima*) are especially sweet. The young leaves, particularly of the **MUSK ROSE** (*R. moschata*) and the **JAPANESE ROSE** (*R. multiflora*), usually reddish in color, are eaten raw or steamed with rice in the East Indies.

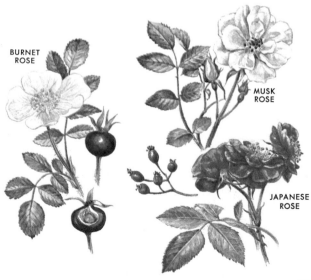

BURNET ROSE

MUSK ROSE

JAPANESE ROSE

GREAT
BURNET

SALAD
BURNET

GREAT BURNET (*Sanguisorba officinalis,* syn. *Poterium officinale*) occurs wild from Japan to Iran and diagonally across Europe to Iceland. It is cultivated in temperate and mild climates. A perennial herb (1-3½ ft. tall), it has a thick, erect stem and compound leaves (the largest leaflets ¾-1½ in. long), bluish-green beneath. The juice of the leaves and roots was often employed to stanch bleeding in medieval times. **SALAD BURNET,** or **LESSER BURNET** (*Sanguisorba minor,* syn. *Poterium sanguisorba*), is indigenous to and very common in the British Isles and extends through central and southern Europe to Morocco and Iran; it is cultivated in North American gardens. It is a slightly hairy herb (1-2½ ft.) with leaflets ¼-¾ in. long. The burnets are evergreen, except in very severe winters. The crushed leaves smell and taste like cucumber, and are often sprinkled as garnishes on wine and beer and other tankard beverages. Dried leaves may be steeped for tea, and are also added to vinegar. Young shoots of both great and salad burnet are much used in salads, cooked with potherbs and soups, and chopped in cottage and cream cheeses. Burnets are propagated by root division or from seeds, which remain viable for 3 years. Best growth is made in dry sandy soil in full sun. The leaves may be cut continually for a steady supply; new shoots will be freely produced if the plants are kept trimmed to 6 in. and not allowed to flower.

DROPWORT (*Filipendula vulgaris*, syn. *F. hexapetala*) grows wild throughout the British Isles, Europe, Asia, and North Africa, and is cultivated in American gardens. It is a hardy perennial herb (2-3 ft. high) with handsome fernlike leaves (6-18 in. long, leaflets to 1 in. long). The flowers are scentless. Some varieties are highly ornamental. Young leaves are added to soups and salads. The tubers were formerly roasted and eaten in Sweden in times of food shortage. Propagated from seeds and by division of the ovoid tubers attached to the roots. The plant thrives in fairly dry chalky soil, in full sun.

MEADOWSWEET (*Filipendula ulmaria*), also called **QUEEN-OF-THE-MEADOW**, is native from arctic Russia to Iceland, south to Spain and Asia Minor. It is a wetland plant (2-4 ft. tall) with crinkled, compound, dark-green leaves, usually downy-white beneath, and with sweetly scented flowers. All parts of the plant are fragrant and of agreeable flavor; meadowsweet was commonly strewn on floors of homes and public places in early England. The flowers or leaves or both are often used to flavor herb beers and claret wine. A tea is made from the dried plant and sweetened with honey. The leaves are used to sweeten other herb teas. Meadowsweet is grown from seeds in sun or partial shade. *Spiraea alba*, a shrub native to northeastern United States, is also called meadowsweet and queen-of-the-meadow, but is solely ornamental.

DROPWORT

MEADOWSWEET

GERANIACEAE (Geranium Family)

GERANIUMS (species of *Pelargonium*) are perennial herbs, mainly from South and East Africa, cultivated principally in temperate regions, less easily in subtropical climates. There are about 230 species and many hybrids grown mainly for their lovely flowers. Some with scented leaves have been prized for generations for enhancing home cookery. There are now over 200 named varieties in cultivation. Foremost among them are several forms of the ROSE GERANIUM (*P. graveolens*), growing 3-4 ft. high with rough, gray-green leaves (1-4 in. wide), having an aroma of rose and rue, or rose and balsam. One variety of this species, the CAMPHOR ROSE, has a camphor scent. The PEPPERMINT GERA-NIUM (*P. tomentosum*), a hairy, erect, shrubby plant (to 3 ft.) has downy grayish leaves (to 4 in. wide) with a pronounced peppermint odor. LEMON GE-RANIUM (*P. limoneum*) has soft foliage with lemon or balm fragrance. It is assumed to be a hybrid, partly derived from the pink-flowered, lemon-scented *P. crispum*. The NUTMEG GERA-NIUM (*P. fragrans*), with leaves of rose and tansy scent, is thought to be a hybrid of the APPLE GERANIUM (*P. odoratissimum*), which has apple-scented leaves covered with a felt of grayish hairs, and the pennyroyal-scented *P. exstipulatum*, which has small velvety leaves and small white flowers. The leaves of all of these are put in potpourri, and are used to

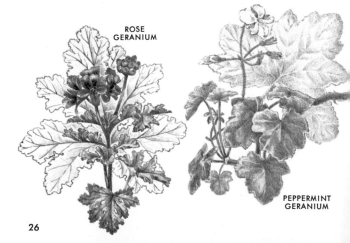

ROSE
GERANIUM

PEPPERMINT
GERANIUM

flavor jellies and desserts. Some cooks put a leaf in the bottom of a cake pan. Some scented geraniums are suggestive of pine, others of apricot and coconut. However, not all *Pelargonium* species have pleasant aromas; the red-flowered varieties most commonly grown as ornamental plants are believed to have largely stemmed from the **FISH GERANIUM** (*P. inquinans*), the velvety foliage of which has a distinctly fishy aroma. Geranium oil, important in the manufacture of perfume, is distilled not only from the pleasingly fragrant *P. graveolens*, *P. fragrans*, *P. crispum*, *P. odoratissimum*, *P. exstipulatum*, and the rose-scented *P. capitatum*, but also from *P. quercifolium* and *P. glutinosum*, both with unappealing labdanum odor, from the pungent *P. radens*

(formerly *P. radula*), from *P. vitifolium*, which smells like citronella, and from *P. fulgidum*, which is classed as scentless. Rose geranium oil is produced commercially and utilized by the food industry in beverages, ice cream, candy, baked goods, gelatins, chewing gum, and jellies. Dried leaves of the **HORSESHOE GERANIUM** (*P. zonale*) are sold by herb vendors in Cuba and steeped to make a tea regarded as a tonic. Scented geraniums are easily grown from cuttings (3-5 in. long) of young short-jointed shoots. In warm, but not hot, climates they do well outside in the sun the year around, if not subjected to heavy rains. To discourage too rapid growth, they should be allowed to bloom only in early spring and kept pinched back the rest of the time.

NUTMEG GERANIUM

P. crispum minor   P. crispum

OXALIDACEAE (Wood Sorrel Family)

WOOD SORREL (*Oxalis violacea*), native over most of the United States and some of the West Indies, is a creeping perennial (4-10 in. high) sometimes cultivated in rock or herb gardens. The acid leaves are eaten alone or used in sandwiches and salads, as are those of the **WOOD SORREL** (*O. acetosella*) of Europe, the universal **YELLOW SORREL** (*O. corniculata*), the **SOURSOB** (*O. pescaprae*) of South Africa and Australia, and the **CHULCO** (*O. pubescens*) in Colombia. High oxalic acid content makes these plants toxic in quantity.

WOOD SORREL

NASTURTIUM

TROPAEOLACEAE (Nasturtium Family)

NASTURTIUM, or **INDIAN CRESS** (*Tropaeolum majus*), from Peru and cultivated for over 300 years, is a climbing herb with smooth leaves (2-7 in. wide) and flowers of varied hue. The dwarf *T. minus* is similar but the lower petals are spotted. The peppery young leaves are eaten in salads. They lavishly garnished the cold dish salmagundi of a former era. Buds and unripe seedpods are often pickled as a substitute for capers. Ripe, dried seeds are ground and used as seasoning. Crushed flowers are steeped in spiced vinegar and the strained mixture used as a sauce. Blossoms stuffed with herbs, capers, and tuna fish are served as hors d'oeuvres. Grown quickly from seeds in full sun.

RUTACEAE (Rue Family)

BROWN BORONIA (*Boronia megastima*), wild in western Australia and cultivated commercially near Melbourne, is a perennial herb (to 2 ft. in sun; shrubby, to 6 ft. in shade). The leaves are compound, faintly downy. The plant is cherished in gardens for the fragrance of its flowers. Their essential oil, sold as Boronia Absolute, smells of cinnamon and tobacco and is valued in perfumes. In food manufacturing, it is employed to create a black currant flavor and to enrich other fruit flavors in beverages, ice creams, candy, and baked goods. Grown from seeds soaked in hot water 4 days; transplanted when very young. Needs moist acid soil and wind protection. Should be cut back after blooming.

FRAXINELLA (*Dictamnus albus*), also known as **GAS PLANT, BURNING BUSH**, or **DITTANY**, native from southern Europe to China, is a semi-woody perennial (2-3 ft. tall) with glossy compound leaves (leaflets 1-3 in. long). The showy flowers may be rose-violet, pink, or white. Flowers and foliage are pleasingly fragrant, with either a lemon or vanilla-and-almond scent. The blooming plant emits a volatile oil that can be ignited with a match when the air is dry and still. The dried leaves, steeped, make a pleasant tea. Grown from seeds in full sun. Contact with the seedpods and subsequent exposure to sunlight may cause skin irritation.

BROWN BORONIA

FRAXINELLA

29

RUE

SWEET
VIOLET

RUE, or **HERB OF GRACE** (*Ruta graveolens*), native to Mediterranean Europe, is an attractive, nearly evergreen, bushy perennial (2-3 ft. tall). Leaves are compound (3-5 in. long, with divisions ⅛-½ in. long), sometimes white-edged. Often mentioned in literature, rue was commonly grown by ancient Greeks and Romans as a healing and flavoring plant. The odor is strong, somewhat disagreeable; taste is pungent and bitter. Fresh or dried minced leaves used sparingly in stews, salads, sandwiches, and vegetable juices, and to season cheese and chicken. Oil has been used in commercial flavorings and perfume; is toxic in large doses. Plant is insect repellent and may irritate sensitive skin. Grown from seeds or cuttings, or by root division. Makes sturdiest growth in poor soil, full sun. Flowers in 2 or 3 years; in bloom all summer.

VIOLACEAE (Violet Family)

SWEET VIOLET (*Viola odorata*), native to Europe, Africa, and Asia, and widely cultivated, is a low perennial with downy leaves (1-2 in. wide). In Victorian days the young leaves were dipped in batter and fried, and also used to garnish salads. The fragrant blossoms were used as garnishes, or added to gelatins, ices, vinegar, and salad dressing, or made into syrup or marmalade. The leaf extract is important in perfumes and flavoring ice cream, candy, and baked goods. Grown from seeds, cuttings, or by division.

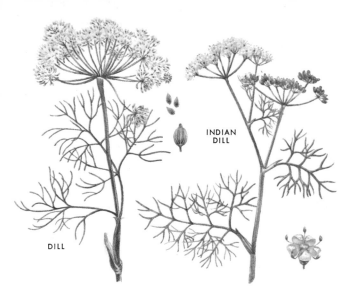

INDIAN DILL

DILL

UMBELLIFERAE (Parsley Family)

DILL (*Anethum graveolens*), native to southern Europe, widely naturalized and cultivated in cool and warm climates, is an annual or biennial herb (2-3 ft. high) with finely cut foliage. Prominent as a medicinal and food plant since A.D. 1000, it is highly aromatic and pungent. Young leaves, fresh or dried, are used in salads, soups, sauces, and dressings, and for seasoning meats, poultry, fish, seafood, and eggs. Seeds are used to flavor pickles, soups, gravies, and breads. Dill oil is important commercially in pickles, condiments, meat products, chewing gum, and candy. Grown from seeds; cuttable in 6 weeks.

INDIAN DILL (*Anethum sowa*) grows wild throughout India and is extensively cultivated in that country and Japan. It is an erect annual (2-4 ft. high), with a downy-white stem and very finely divided leaves. The fresh foliage is eaten with steamed rice and used for flavoring soups, but the seeds are more popular. Although pungent and bitter, they are an essential ingredient in curry powder and are commonly marketed for medicinal use. The distilled seed oil, which resembles that from parsley seed, is also important in the local pharmaceutical trade. In Indonesia the seeds are utilized in pastries and a beverage.

ANGELICA

AMERICAN
ANGELICA

ANGELICA (*Angelica archangelica*), native from Greenland to central Russia and naturalized over most of Europe, is a stout herb (3-7 ft. or more) with compound leaves (2-3 ft. wide). All parts are aromatic and taste of licorice. Leaf midribs may be eaten like celery. Leafstalks and hollow flower stalks, while young, are cut up and preserved in syrup, or candied. Seed extract and essential oils from the root and stem are used to flavor ice cream, candy, baked goods, puddings, syrup, and spirits. Root oil is a valued attractant in insect control. Seed oil is used in toothpaste and perfume. Grown from seeds in shade. Blooms the third year and dies unless flower stalk is cut early.

AMERICAN ANGELICA (*Angelica atropurpurea*), which grows wild in wet fields from Newfoundland to Minnesota and south to West Virginia, is a biennial herb (4-6 ft. or higher) with dark-purple, hollow stem and compound leaves (the lower ones to 2 ft. wide). Entire plant is aromatic and of strong, pungent, somewhat bitter flavor. Young stems and leafstalks are peeled and eaten raw in salads; are milder if cooked in two waters. Leaves are added when cooking fish and put into soups and stews. Tender roots and shoots are candied. Grown from seeds, in semishade. Blooms the second year but best kept from flowering. Was popular in early American herb gardens.

CHERVIL

CELERY

CHERVIL (*Anthriscus cereifolium*), indigenous from central Russia to Iran, is grown in all temperate climates. It is an annual herb (1-2 ft. high) with compound leaves, slightly downy beneath. The plant is aniselike in fragrance and flavor, with a peppery tang. It is especially popular in France and included in all *fines herbes* mixtures. Young leaves give zest to green and potato salads and are used to garnish meats and fish; fresh or dried, they are added to soups, omelets, and stuffings, and are standard in sauces for poultry and chops. Grown from seeds in full sun; ready for cutting in 6 to 8 weeks; stays green all winter. Goes to seed in summer and must be replanted.

CELERY (*Apium graveolens* var. *dulce*) is the improved form of **SMALLAGE**, a weed (1-2 ft.), acrid in flavor and reputedly toxic, of Europe, North Africa, and Asia. Cultivated celery is milder and usually classed as a vegetable. The stalks are mainly used raw as appetizers or in salads, or cooked as flavoring in soups, stews, and casseroles. The leaves, more potent in flavor, are chopped with the stalks for celery soup and are much used in Chinese dishes; in Indonesia they are mixed with steamed rice. Celery seed, seed extract, and oil are commercially important in beverages, celery salt and other condiments, meats, soups, pickles, and bakery products.

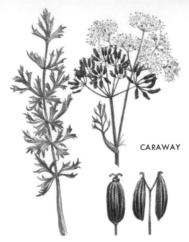

CARAWAY

PARSLEY

CARAWAY (*Carum carvi*), native to north and central Europe and widely naturalized and cultivated in temperate regions, is an erect biennial herb (to 2 ft.) with ferny foliage and slender, yellow root (to 8 in. long). In Germany and Switzerland, the root is boiled, as it was many centuries ago. Fresh leaves, used as a garnish, add flavor to vegetables. The seeds are popular on cookies and cakes and much consumed in rye bread and cheese. They are often colorfully sugar-coated and eaten as a confection. The seed oil is utilized in ice cream, candy, bakery products, meat, pickles, condiments, soft drinks, and alcoholic beverages. Caraway is the basis of the liqueur kümmel and the Scandinavian brandy schnapps. Grows from seeds; blooms the second year; reseeds itself.

PARSLEY (*Petroselinum crispum*), wild in north and central Europe, is more common in home gardens the world over than any other herb. It is a short-lived perennial (1½-2 ft. high) with more or less curly compound leaves. There are many varieties, including one with a thick root which is cooked as a vegetable. Fresh sprigs of parsley are unequaled as garnish but, fortunately, rarely eaten, for parsley is harmful in quantity. Fresh chopped or dried and powdered, leaves have endless uses as seasoning in sauces, dressings, croquettes, egg, fish, shellfish, and meat dishes. Parsley herb oil and the seed oil are employed in commercial preparation of sauces, pickles, meats, bakery products, and soups. The seed oil is also used in perfumes for men. Grown from seeds. Needs rich, moist soil.

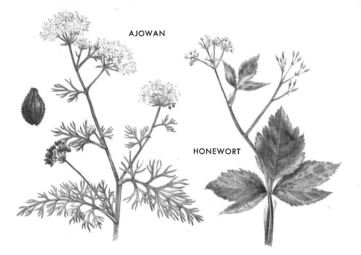

AJOWAN

HONEWORT

AJOWAN, or **AJWAIN** (*Carum copticum,* syn. *Ptychotis ajowan*), native to Asia Minor and nearby Africa, is cultivated in Egypt, Iran, Afghanistan, and India; also in Montserrat and the Seychelles. It is a faintly hairy annual herb (1-3½ ft. high) with finely divided compound leaves. Grown mainly for its aromatic, pungent seeds, in great demand as seasoning in curries and other dishes, and considered a good preservative for canned foods. In India, ajowan oil, sweeter than oil of thyme, is extracted from both the plant and the seeds for flavoring and pharmaceutical use. Seeds are much used medicinally, and were formerly a source of the antiseptic thymol now produced synthetically. **AJMUD** (*C. roxburghianum*) is similar. Its leaves are substituted for parsley and its seeds are put into curries.

HONEWORT (*Cryptotaenia canadensis*), also called **JAPANESE WILD CHERVIL** and **MITSUBA,** is native from Manitoba to New Brunswick south to Georgia and Texas, and also in China, North Vietnam, and Japan. It is cultivated as a culinary herb in Japan and by Japanese in Indonesia and Hawaii. In China it is prominent in herbal medicine. It is an erect, succulent perennial (1-3½ ft. high), developing a thick, creeping rootstock with very long, stringy roots and a pungent, celerylike odor. Leaves are trifoliate (leaflets 2½-4 in. long). Young leaves taste much like those of celery; are cooked as greens or served cold with soy sauce. The hollow leafstalks are added to soups, salads, and fried foods. Grown from seeds or by division; needs rich soil and shade. Planted successively for continual supply.

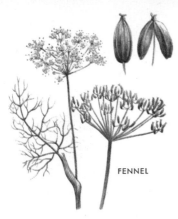

FENNEL

LOVAGE

FENNEL (*Foeniculum vulgare*), from southern Europe and western Asia, is widely grown in mild and warm climates. A stout perennial herb (4-6 ft.) with wispy foliage, aromatic, and of warm, sweetish taste, its history as a medicinal and food plant goes back to early Egypt. Young leaves are used as garnish and to season soups, salads, and fish. Seeds, whole or ground, are much used at home and commercially in cookies, cakes, cheese, fish, meat, and vegetables. A dwarf variety, **FINNOCHIO**, or **FLORENCE FENNEL** (*F. dulce*), has large leaf bases cooked as a vegetable. Young stems of another variety, **CAROSELLA** (*F. piperitum*), are eaten raw. Oil from common (bitter) fennel is valued in flavoring liqueurs and in household sprays to mask odors. Sweet fennel oil is used in brandy (anisette), candy, cough drops, and ice cream. Grown from seeds.

LOVAGE (*Levisticum officinale*, syn. *Ligusticum levisticum*), native to alpine France and Italy and cultivated in cold climates, is a handsome perennial herb (to 6 ft.) with glossy compound leaves and thick brown root. Entire plant has a celery-and-parsley odor. Chopped young leaves are put into salads, soups, stews, and seafood dishes. Leafstalks may be blanched and eaten like celery, or candied. The seeds, which resemble those of caraway, are used whole or ground in candy, cakes, and meat cookery, and are sometimes pickled like capers. In the food industry, dried leaves and the potent extract and oil from the fresh plant are used in beverages, condiments, icings, and syrups. The strong oil of the root is used in the manufacture of liqueurs, tobacco, and heavy, spicy perfumes. Grown by division or from seeds. Lovage does best in moist soil and full sun.

CORIANDER

CULANTRO

CORIANDER (*Coriandrum sativum*), of eastern Mediterranean origin and universally cultivated, has a long history of use, seeds having been found in 9th- and 10th-century Egyptian tombs. It is an attractive annual herb (to 2 ft. tall). The fernlike foliage and globular seeds have a "bedbug" odor when fresh. Nevertheless, the herb is very popular, especially in the Orient. Young leaves are added to salads, soups, and curries. Dried leaves and seeds are pleasantly aromatic and of sweet but pungent flavor. The seeds are enjoyed sugar-coated. Coriander seed oil is commercially important in flavoring hard candy, fruits, sausages and other meats, baked goods, cheese, pickles, condiments, alcoholic beverages (especially gin and vermouth), and tobacco. It is highly valued in perfumes and colognes. Grows readily from seeds in full sun and lime-rich soil.

CULANTRO (*Eryngium foetidum*), native to tropical America and the West Indies and introduced into cultivation in the Orient, is a perennial herb with spiny-toothed leaves (2-8 in. long) and a "bedbug" odor like that of coriander but stronger. In fact, culantro is the Spanish word for coriander. To distinguish culantro (*E. foetidum*) from coriander (*C. sativum*), West Indian cooks tag the name *culantro* with *de burro, del monte, de coyote,* or *de cimarron.* English names are fitweed, stinkweed, and Java coriander. Traditionally indispensable in Colombian, Peruvian, Panamanian, and Cuban cuisine, culantro was adopted long ago for culinary use by the Chinese, Indonesians, and other peoples of Southeast Asia. Young leaves are used as garnish for fish and as flavoring in soups and curries; they are also eaten with rice. Grows rapidly from seeds.

ANISE (*Pimpinella anisum*), indigenous from Greece to Egypt and grown in warm climates of the Old and New Worlds, is an annual, finely hairy herb (to 2½ ft.) with feathery foliage and slender seeds, both having a sweet, characteristic odor and flavor. In many countries, anise is esteemed as much for its medicinal properties as for its culinary value. The chopped fresh leaves are appealing in soups, stews, sauces, and salads. Anise seed is much used in meat products, condiments, bakery goods, and liqueurs, such as muscatel, vermouth, anisette, and Turkish raki. Traditionally the distilled oil has been used to flavor licorice candy, cough drops, chewing gum, ice cream, pickles, and tobacco and as an odor-masker. Recently, natural anise oil has been giving way to synthetic anethole. Grows readily from seeds. Blooms appear in 10 weeks.

BURNET SAXIFRAGE (*Pimpinella saxifraga*), which occurs wild in the British Isles and most of Europe and Asia Minor, is a slender perennial herb (1-3½ ft.) with a rough stem and variously shaped leaves. Young leaves and shoots have a cucumber odor; are eaten in salads; have been tied in bundles and hung in casks of beer, ale, and wine to improve the flavor. Flower heads were formerly made into wine and sugar-coated seeds eaten as a confection. Root has strong, disagreeable odor and biting, bitter taste. Its essential oil is used in pharmaceutical products and to flavor candy and liqueurs. **GREATER BURNET SAXIFRAGE** (*P. major*, syn. *P. magna*), of similar range, is a larger plant (to 4 ft.) with a ridged or angled stem. The root serves the same purposes as that of the smaller species. A rose-flowered variety is grown in English rock gardens. Both species like shade.

ANISE

BURNET SAXIFRAGE

SWEET CICELY (*Myrrhis odorata*), also called **FERN-LEAVED CHERVIL,** is found wild on European mountains and is common in parts of the British Isles, but little known elsewhere except in Chile. It is a somewhat hairy perennial (2-4 ft.) with soft, silky foliage and thick taproot (to 2 ft. long). The plant has a strong but agreeable odor and sugary, aniselike flavor. The flowers are sweet-scented. Young leaves are popular as flavoring in French cookery, in soups and stews. They are chopped with tarragon in butter for garnishing steaks and chops. Seeds are spicy additions to salads and are used to flavor Chartreuse. They were formerly used in northern England to scent and polish oak. The root is boiled and eaten cold with vinegar and oil. The plant is rubbed inside hives to attract honeybees. Propagated from seeds, which take months to germinate.

SWEET CICELY

WINTERGREEN

ERICACEAE
(Heath Family)

WINTERGREEN (*Gaultheria procumbens*), also known as **CHECKERBERRY** or **TEABERRY,** is found wild from Newfoundland to Manitoba, and south to Minnesota and the mountains of Georgia. It is a dwarf plant (4-8 in. tall) with evergreen, leathery leaves (¾-2 in. long). The fruit, present all winter, is edible and was formerly marketed in New England. Aromatic, tender new leaves are a popular nibble. Young or old leaves make a very agreeable tea. Oil from the dried leaves was formerly important in flavoring birch beer, candy, chewing gum, and toothpaste, and in blending perfume, but has been largely replaced by the synthetic methyl salicylate. True wintergreen oil is still used to flavor pharmaceutical preparations. Easily grown from seeds or cuttings in moist, acid soil and partial shade.

39

BORAGINACEAE (Borage Family)

BORAGE (*Borago officinalis*), a native of central and Mediterranean Europe and North Africa, is occasionally grown in the United States, Australia, India, the West Indies, and Latin America. It is an annual or biennial herb (1½-2 ft. high) with hairy stems and leaves (to 4-6 in. long). The plant is noted for its cucumber odor and flavor. In times past, flowers were candied and young leaves and flowers were used as a garnish, in salads, in a mixture of ale, wine, and brandy, or in a cool drink of cider, water, lemon juice, and various herbs. Today it is mainly an ornamental and folk-medicine plant. Some varieties have white or purple flowers or variegated leaves. Grown from seeds in dry soil and full sun.

COMFREY (*Symphytum officinale*), native from the British Isles to Siberia and south to Spain and Turkey, is a hairy perennial (1-4 ft. high) with soft leaves (6-8 in. long), sometimes variegated, a thick root, and white, yellow, pink, or purple flowers. Young shoots eaten as greens; mature leaves formerly used to flavor cakes and a sauce base known as panada. The root, sweetish and mucilaginous, has been much used in folk medicine. The dried, pulverized leaves and root are imported and sold in the United States for steeping as herb tea. Grown from seeds in moist soil. It is cultivated as an herb mainly by natural-food enthusiasts, but varieties with vivid blooms are popular as ornamentals.

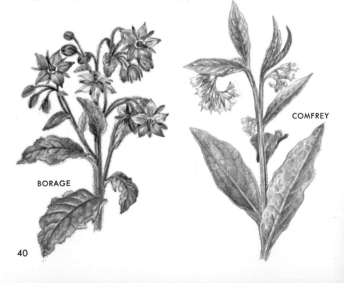

COMFREY

BORAGE

VERBENACEAE (Vervain Family)

MEXICAN OREGANO (*Lippia graveolens*, syn. *L. berlandieri*), of southern Mexico, is a shrub (3½-8 ft.) with aromatic, crinkled leaves, downy-white beneath. It is common in local gardens, and the leaves are much used for flavoring fish, sausages, and other foods, especially *pozole* (pork and hominy), and for tea. Dried leaves of this plant and of *L. palmeri*, of Sonora and Baja California, are exported to the United States as "oregano." They are not differentiated in the trade from the oregano of Europe (see Wild Marjoram, page 66) and are used in the same ways. Several other species of *Lippia* are locally known as oregano in Latin America and the West Indies and esteemed in cookery and as medicinal herbs. One of the most widely distributed, popular in India as well as the American tropics, is *Lippia alba*. Its fresh leaves have a delightful lemongrass odor and are prized for flavoring soup, meats, and fish and for making a pleasant tea. In Puerto Rico, *L. helleri* is used as a condiment and its essential oil is used in liqueurs and toilet products. **FALSE THYME** (*L. micromera*), which gets its name from its thyme-scented leaves, grows wild in the West Indies and is cultivated in Trinidad and Hawaii for flavoring food. *L. adoensis*, of the Congo, is the source of the popular Gambian bush tea. The leaves of *L. pseudo-thea* are used for tea in Brazil. All species grow from cuttings or seeds.

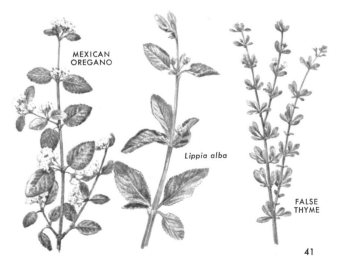

MEXICAN OREGANO

Lippia alba

FALSE THYME

LEMON VERBENA

LEMON VERBENA (*Aloysia triphylla*, syn. *Lippia citriodora*), from Argentina and Chile, is widely grown in home gardens in Mediterranean Europe, Africa, India, and other mild climates and in greenhouses in cold regions. It is a shrubby plant (3-10 ft.) with lemon-scented leaves (2-3 in. long). Fresh leaves are most prized for herb tea. They are also used as garnish, and to flavor cold drinks, fruit cups, salads, jellies, and desserts. Verbena oil, formerly distilled from the leaves for use in perfumes and flavoring of soft drinks and liqueurs, is expensive and has been largely replaced by lemongrass and other essential oils with similar properties. Leaves dried for sachets lose their scent in six months. Usually grown from cuttings; does well potted.

LABIATAE, the **MINT FAMILY**, is the most prominent herb family, embracing the hyssops, lavenders, thymes, sages, basils, and others, as well as the "true" mints.

PERILLA (*Perilla frutescens*), from mountain areas of India, China, and Japan, is an ornamental annual herb (1½-4 ft.) with cinnamon-scented leaves (2-6 in. long), bronze-purple, or green mottled with purple, red, pink, or white. Fresh or pickled leaves, seedlings, or seeds give savor to raw fish, bean curd, sliced cucumbers, pickles, and tempura. Leaves of a variety, *crispa*, are used to color preserved ginger and fruits. Volatile oil from leaves and flowering tops of this variety is a flavoring for sauces, candy, and toothpaste, and is used in perfumes. Perillaldehyde, derived from the oil, is 2,000 times sweeter than sucrose and 4-8 times sweeter than saccharin; it is used to sweeten tobacco. Perilla seeds yield a drying oil for paints, varnishes, enamels, inks, and linoleum. Grown from seeds, which must be prechilled.

PERILLA

LAVENDER (*Lavandula officinalis*), from the mountains of southern France, is widely grown in temperate and mild climates. It is a shrubby plant (to 3 or 4 ft.) with grayish, downy leaves (1½-2 in. long) and delightfully fragrant flowers which, in former times, were candied. Today, they are used to garnish fruit cups, and the leaves, petals, and budding tips are added to salads, dressings, jellies, wine, and soft drinks. In food manufacturing, essential oil distilled from the flowering tops and stalks is employed in flavoring beverages, ice cream, candy, baked goods, and chewing gum. It is an old favorite for scenting soaps, colognes, and other toilet products. Since ancient times, dried lavender has been prized for scenting clothing and linens. **SPIKE LAVENDER** (*L. latifolia*), from low altitudes in Mediterranean areas, and cultivated commercially in Spain, is similar but has broader leaves and less fragrant flowers. It yields camphorlike oil used primarily in soaps. **LAVANDIN**, a hybrid between common lavender and spike lavender, is cultivated at low altitudes mainly in southern France. It is easy to grow and yields more oil than its parents and is replacing them as an industrial source of essential oil. **TOPPED LAVENDER**, or **FRENCH LAVENDER** (*L. stoechas*), of southwestern Europe, is an herb (2-3 ft. high) with very narrow, downy, gray leaves (½-1¼ in. long) and showy flowers used in sachets and for perfume. The essential oil has a camphor-rosemary odor; it is used medicinally in ointments and liniments and as a moth repellent.

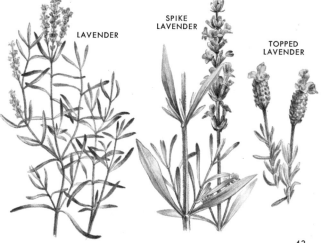

LAVENDER

SPIKE LAVENDER

TOPPED LAVENDER

43

INDIAN BORAGE (*Coleus amboinicus*), known as **SPANISH THYME**, and as **OREGANO** in Manila, Aruba, Yucatan, and Cuba, is of unknown origin but grown in home gardens in the tropics. It is a perennial herb (to 3 ft. high) with thick stems and fleshy leaves (2-4 in. long) of strong aroma and flavor. Leaf bits are added to salads and used as seasoning in cooking black beans, goat meat, and strong-smelling fish and shellfish. Europeans in India use the leaves in wine and beer. Leaves are steeped for tea and in Indonesia are rubbed on the hair and clothes after bathing. Grows readily from cuttings.

BETONY (*Stachys officinalis*), also called **WOOD BETONY** and **BISHOP'S WORT**, is native to the British Isles, temperate Europe, and Algeria. It is a slightly hairy perennial herb (½-2 ft. high) with rough leaves (1-4 in. long) and red-purple, rose, or white flowers. The plant, esteemed by the ancients as a cure-all, has a somewhat bitter and salty flavor. A weak infusion (1 oz. dried betony to 1 pt. boiling water) is considered an excellent substitute for tea. The related species, *S. heraclea*, is similarly esteemed in Greece, and *S. rugosa* in southern Africa. Fresh plant reputedly intoxicating; dried plant may cause sneezing.

BETONY

INDIAN BORAGE

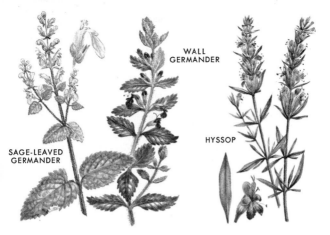

WALL
GERMANDER

HYSSOP

SAGE-LEAVED
GERMANDER

SAGE-LEAVED GERMANDER (*Teucrium scorodonia*), also called **WOOD SAGE**, is common in the British Isles and from Norway to northern Italy and central Spain. It is a downy perennial herb (½-2 ft. high) with crinkled leaves (1¼-3 in. long). The plant has a pronounced odor like that of hops and the leaves and flowers are very bitter. A strong infusion called Ambroise has been much used in France and the Channel Islands as a substitute for hops in flavoring ale. In rural England it was similarly added to homemade beer. **WALL GERMANDER** (*T. chamaedrys*), from central and southern Europe and Morocco, is a perennial, hairy, semiwoody herb growing in tufts (8-10 in. high). Its glossy dark-green leaves (to 1¼ in. long) are scentless unless crushed. Grown by division, mainly as an ornamental.

HYSSOP (*Hyssopus officinalis*), native to mountainous areas of southern Europe, western Asia, and Morocco, and commercially cultivated in Europe, is a semiwoody perennial plant (8 in. to 2 ft. high) with nearly evergreen leaves (⅝-1 in. long). Flowers usually blue, sometimes red or white. Plant has an agreeable camphor-mint odor and pungent, bitterish taste. The young shoots were formerly used to season soups, salads, sauces, pickles, and meats. Today the essential oil is employed for those purposes and for flavoring bitters and alcoholic beverages, especially liqueurs like chartreuse. The oil is also important in perfumery. A hot poultice of the mashed plant is an old-time remedy for a "black eye." Biblical hyssop is not this plant, but has been identified as Syrian marjoram (*Origanum maru*).

45

KOREAN
MINT

ANISE
HYSSOP

KOREAN MINT (*Agastache rugosa*, syn. *Lophanthus rugosus*), indigenous to and cultivated in Korea, Japan, eastern China, and highlands of North Vietnam, was introduced into the United States in 1947 and thrives in temperate areas. It is a bushy perennial herb (3-4 ft. high) with deeply veined leaves (2 in. long, 1¼ in. wide), finely hairy on both sides. The plant is aniselike in odor and flavor. Fresh or dried leaves are used to season meats and dressings and are steeped for tea. In China, an infusion of the stems and leaves is employed as a mouthwash, and as an antidote for overindulgence in wine. Grown from seeds; does well in sunny locations.

ANISE HYSSOP (*Agastache foeniculum*, syns. *A. anisata, A. anethiodora*) was formerly found wild throughout the north central United States and ranging up to Manitoba, but now appears mainly in cultivation. It is an attractive perennial herb (3-4 ft. tall) with nearly smooth leaves (to 3½ in. long), whitish and faintly downy on the underside. They smell strongly of anise. American Indians made much use of this plant for tea. The leaves can be used fresh or dried for culinary seasoning. It is widely grown as a honey plant as its flowers, which bloom from early summer until October, produce copious nectar eagerly sought by bees and yielding a light, fragrant honey. Wild birds are fond of the seeds. Propagated from seeds, it grows very slowly at the outset; needs full sun.

MEXICAN GIANT HYSSOP (*Agastache mexicana*), from northern Mexico, and cultivated in temperate-zone gardens, is a perennial herb (to 2½ ft.) with a creeping rootstock and somewhat downy leaves (to 2½ in. long). The entire plant is highly aromatic, and the young leaves are useful for flavoring and for tea. Indians of Arizona made similar use of *A. pallidiflora* subsp. *neomexicana*, which is a hardier plant, ranging up to altitudes of 9,500 feet. All of the giant hyssops are extremely attractive to honeybees and are often grown by beekeepers. Giant hyssops are grown from seeds or by division; need protection in winter.

NINDI, or **NINDE**, is the local and trade name for *Aeolanthus graveolens*, *A. nyrianthus*, *A. heliotropioides*, *A. pubescens*, *A. lamborayi*, and several other species native and cultivated in Nigeria, Uganda, Tanzania, Gabon, and Northern Rhodesia. They are creeping herbs, of rocky ground, with more or less fleshy leaves (to 2 in. long) and of strong, agreeable, basil-like odor and flavor. The leaves are esteemed in salads and soups, and steeped to make a medicinal tea. In recent years, the plants have been used as new sources of fragrance; factories have been built in East Africa for distilling the essential oil from the entire herb for use in soaps and perfumes. The oil has an appealing rose-lemon aroma; rose scent is mainly in the flowers, lemon in the leaves.

MEXICAN GIANT HYSSOP

NINDI

CATNIP

CATNIP, or **CATMINT** (*Nepeta cataria*), native from Scandinavia to Kashmir, is widely naturalized and cultivated in temperate climates. It is a perennial herb (1½-5 ft. tall) with downy leaves (1-3 in. long), a strong mint-pennyroyal odor, and pungent, bitter, camphorlike flavor. Leaves and young shoots, fresh or dried, are used to season sauces, soups, and stews. Well known as an excitant for cats. The active principle is the feline sex-attractant; the volatile oil is a lure for trapping members of the cat family. Grown from seeds or cuttings.

GROUND IVY (*Glechoma hederacea;* syn. *Nepeta hederacea*), also known as **GILL-OVER-THE-GROUND** and **ALEHOOF,** occurs wild from the British Isles to Japan. It is a pretty perennial herb (4-12 in. high) with long trailing and rooting stems and soft hairy leaves (½-1¼ in. wide). The plant has a strong, disagreeable odor and bitter flavor. In early England it was added to ale, to clarify it and improve the flavor and keeping-quality. A leaf infusion was much imbibed by the poor as a cheap substitute for tea. Grown in hanging baskets.

GROUND
IVY

HOREHOUND

HOREHOUND (*Marrubium vulgare*) is native to the Mediterranean areas of Europe, Asia, and Africa and the Azores and Canary Islands, and naturalized in England, North America, and Australia. It is a spreading, woolly-white perennial herb (to 2 ft. high) with crinkled leaves (¾-2 in. long). The fresh plant has a musky odor and is bitter and pungent. Leaves used in England and Australia to make nonalcoholic beer and candy. Horehound extract is used commercially, mainly in lozenges. Grown from seeds or cuttings, or by root division.

SANGURA (*Hyptis suaveolens*), also called **BUSH TEA BUSH** and **WILD SPIKENARD**, is native to tropical America, naturalized in the Old World tropics, and commonly grown in home gardens. It is an erect, coarse herb (1½-7 ft. tall) with soft, pleasantly aromatic leaves (to 4½ in. long). Very young tips are used for food seasoning. In West Africa and the West Indies the leaf infusion is enjoyed as a beverage. Dried leaves are occasional adulterants of patchouli (see page 152). In Mexico the seeds are made into gruel.

SANGURA

FIELD
MINT

FIELD MINT, or **CORN MINT** (*Mentha arvensis*), is native from the British Isles and Scandinavia to Spain and central Italy and from temperate northern Asia to the Himalayas, and is occasionally cultivated in home gardens. It is a more or less erect herb (4 in. to 2 ft. high) with downy or hairless leaves (1-2 in. long) of strong odor and flavor; it is not as popular as milder mints. This plant is one of the parents of several hybrids. **JAPANESE MINT** (*M. arvensis* subsp. *haplocalyx* var. *piperascens*), extensively cultivated in Japan and on a lesser scale in China and Brazil, is a velvety, erect plant (2-3 ft. high) with finely hairy leaves (to 4 in. long), yielding Japanese mint oil or Japanese peppermint oil, which is an inferior substitute for true peppermint oil. The plant is also a source of menthol; the dementholized oil is a flavoring for mouthwash and toothpaste. **JAVA MINT** (*M. arvensis* var. *javanica*) is cultivated in the East Indies, the fresh leaves being added to vegetable and rice dishes. Propagation is by means of cuttings or transplanting of rooted suckers.

JAPANESE
MINT

JAVA
MINT

M. X alopecuroides

APPLE MINT, WOOLLY MINT, or **ROUND-LEAVED MINT** (*Mentha rotundifolia*), from central and southern Europe and the Azores and naturalized in North America from Maine to Mexico, is widely cultivated in mild-temperate regions. It is an erect perennial (2-3 ft. tall) with stems thickly covered by grayish or white hairs, and with downy leaves (1-2 in. long), whitish on the underside. Crushed stems have an ether-peppermint odor. The leaves have a delicate applelike aroma and flavor and are used fresh for garnishing drinks and flavoring foods. This mint is considered by connoisseurs to be superior to spearmint for all culinary purposes though its downiness is a deterrent to those unfamiliar with its fine flavor. **PINEAPPLE MINT** (var. *variegata*) (to 10 in. high) has smaller, white-blotched leaves, and its young tips have a distinct pineapple odor. Among many hybrids between *M. rotundifolia* and *M. longifolia* is *M. X alopecuroides*, a sturdy plant (2-5 ft. high) with wrinkled, very hairy leaves (1½-3½ in. long), esteemed in England for home use, especially in mint sauce.

APPLE MINT

PINEAPPLE MINT

M. longifolia

51

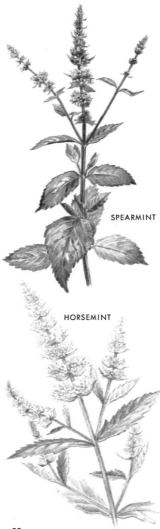

SPEARMINT

HORSEMINT

SPEARMINT (*Mentha X spicata*, syn. *M. viridis*), variously known as **GREEN MINT, BROWN MINT, ROMAN MINT,** or **LAMB MINT,** is supposedly a hybrid between *M. longifolia* and *M. rotundifolia*, wild in the mountains of central Europe and naturalized in the British Isles and much of the United States. It is an erect herb (1-3 ft. tall) with nearly hairless, crinkled leaves (1½-3½ in. long) having a lemon-mint odor and bitter, pungent, camphorous taste. This is the most popular mint of temperate climates for garnishing drinks, fruit cups, and vegetables, for seasoning soups and making mint sauce for roast lamb, and for tea. The dried plant, essential oil, and extract are commercial flavorings for meat products, condiments, soft drinks, ice cream, candy, baked goods, gelatins, mint jelly, chewing gum, and for various alcoholic beverages.

HORSEMINT (*Mentha longifolia*, syns. *M. sylvestris, M. tomentosa*) occurs wild from southern Europe to the Himalayas and is cultivated in temperate climates. It is an erect or sprawling herb (1-4 ft. high), with hairy stems and stemless leaves (2-5 in. long), downy-white on the underside. There is great variation in this species; it is said to include 21 subspecies and 150 types. The fresh plant is used as a seasoning in Indian chutneys. The leaves are candied. Dried leaves and flowering tops yield a volatile oil much like oil of peppermint for which it serves as a substitute in flavoring candy.

PEPPERMINT (*Mentha X piperita*), apparently a hybrid between *M. aquatica* and *M. X spicata*, is cultivated in temperate areas of Europe, North America, Australia, and Asia. It is an erect or spreading, hairless herb (1-3 ft. high) with green or purplish stems and dark, nearly smooth leaves (1-4 in. long), with strong peppermint odor and slightly bitter, camphorous flavor. Fresh young tips and leaves are used for culinary flavoring and have been frequently steeped for tea. In the food industry, the volatile oil is extensively utilized for flavoring candy, chewing gum, soft drinks, ice cream and syrups, baked goods, gelatins, and alcoholic drinks including Benedictine and crème de menthe. It is being increasingly used in soaps and other toilet products, as well as household sprays and pharmaceutical preparations.

YERBA BUENA, or **HIERBA BUENA,** is the Spanish name for *Mentha nemorosa* (syn. *M. sylvestris* var. *nemorosa*), a red-stemmed, glossy-leaved mint grown in home gardens of Cuba, Puerto Rico, and most other West Indian islands. The strongly aromatic leaves and young shoots are used for flavoring soups and meats and are steeped for medicinal tea. The yerba buena of Yucatan is *M. sativa*, indispensable in meat sauces, *morcilla* (a pudding), meatballs, and a spiced wine drink. In Venezuela, "hierba buena" is applied to bergamot mint, peppermint, and spearmint.

PEPPERMINT

YERBA BUENA

WATER MINT, or MARSH MINT (*Mentha aquatica*), grows wild from the British Isles to North Africa and Madeira, and is widely naturalized and cultivated. It is a perennial herb (6 in. to 3 ft. high) with weak stems varying from smooth to hairy, often reddish, and with variable leaves (to 2 in. long), hairy on both sides. It has a strong, distinctive odor and flavor and is used as a seasoning herb, particularly for meat hash in Southeast Asia, and is a tea substitute in southern Africa. **CURLED MINT, or CROSS MINT**, is a crisped form (var. *crispa*, syn. *M. crispa*) with reclining red stems (to 3 ft. long), naturalized in the eastern United States and a favorite in herb gardens. It has a resinous, pinelike odor and is prized for flavoring foods, punch, and liqueurs, and is a source of pharmaceutical German spearmint oil. *M. aquatica* is one of the parents of many hybrids.

BERGAMOT MINT, also called **LEMON MINT** or **ORANGE MINT** and often identified as *Mentha citrata* (syn. *M. odorata*), is believed to be a form of *M. aquatica* that originated in central and southern Europe. It is grown in home gardens in the Bahamas, Cuba, Puerto Rico, the Virgin Islands, and Yucatan. In the United States, it is naturalized and cultivated for commercial purposes, primarily in Washington and Oregon. It is a smooth perennial herb (to 1 ft. high) with reclining, reddish stems (1-2 ft. long) and thin, purple-edged leaves (½-2 in. long). The flowers have an aroma resembling that of lavender. The leaves yield a lemon-scented oil much like true bergamot oil (see page 139) but with certain bitter principles that must be removed before it can be used for food flavoring. The oil is an ingredient in Chartreuse, but its most important use is in perfumes.

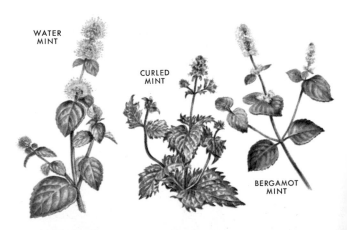

WATER MINT

CURLED MINT

BERGAMOT MINT

AMERICAN
APPLE MINT

ENGLISH
SPEARMINT

AMERICAN APPLE MINT, or RED MINT (Mentha X gentilis, syn. M. cardiaca), a hybrid of M. arvensis and M. X spicata, grows wild in the British Isles, is naturalized in North America from Canada to Georgia and grown commercially in the United States and Australia. It is a perennial herb (1-1½ ft. high) with erect, dark-red or reddish-purple stems. The leaves (1½-2½ in. long) are variable in form and degree of downiness. In the United States this plant is the chief source of "oil of spearmint," used mainly in chewing gum. **GOLDEN MINT** (var. variegata), with spreading stems and leaves blotched with yellow or ivory, has an appealing fruity flavor. The variety gracilis is erect (1-1½ ft. high) and is distinguished by its many short branches.

ENGLISH SPEARMINT (Mentha X villosa-nervata), a hybrid of M. longifolia and M. X spicata, with reddish stems, is the most important mint grown in greenhouses and marketed fresh in England. **HEART-LEAVED MINT** (M. X cordifolia), a cross of M. rotundifolia and M. X spicata, is a vigorous, coarse plant with rounded, wrinkled leaves. It is grown commercially outdoors in southern England.

MINT CULTURE. All of the foregoing mints are perennials with creeping roots and are propagated by root division, or from cuttings. They grow rapidly in moist, rich soil and in full or partial shade. In commercial plantations, the mint fields are plowed up and new root cuttings set out every three years.

SPANISH MINT (*Mentha requienii*), also called **CORSICAN MINT** or **CORSICAN THYME**, is indigenous to Corsica and Sardinia and grown in subtemperate climates. It is a miniature herb with threadlike, finely hairy, creeping stems and tiny leaves (1/16-1/8 in. wide). It is the only mint grown primarily as an ornamental. Forming dense mats, it is a popular ground cover in herb plantings, rock gardens, and in greenhouses. The entire plant has a very strong peppermint odor. As a flavoring, it is used mainly in liqueurs. Propagated by division. Does best in moist, shady locations but can tolerate sun.

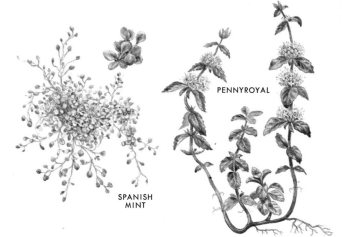

PENNYROYAL

SPANISH
MINT

PENNYROYAL (*Mentha pulegium*), formerly called **PUDDING GRASS**, is native from the British Isles to western Asia and North Africa and cultivated in the Old World and the New. It is a perennial herb (4 in. to 1 ft. high) with reclining stems, often red, and slightly hairy leaves (½-¾ in. long). It has a strong spearmint odor and a pungent, acid taste. In early England, leaves, fresh or dried, were used to season stuffings, meat sauces, stews, and game. The leaves have also been steeped for tea, and strewn in houses to repel fleas. The essential oil plays a small role in perfumery; it is more important in scenting soaps and detergents. The oil from the variety *eriantha* is used to flavor beverages, candy, and baked goods. The variegated variety *gibraltarica* is grown as a ground cover. Propagated by division or cuttings. Forms carpetlike patches.

WESTERN YERBA BUENA (*Micromeria chamissonis*, syn. *M. douglassii*) grows wild from British Columbia to Santa Monica, and is cultivated in temperate North America and in England. It is a perennial herb with long, slender, creeping stems which root at the tips, and sweetly fragrant leaves (to 1 in. long).

American Indians gather the leafy stems, roll them into a ball for drying and later steeping for tea. The village that developed into the city of San Francisco was originally named for this plant. The related *M. juliana* of the Mediterranean region is called savory and was formerly grown in herb gardens.

WESTERN
YERBA
BUENA

BALM

BALM, or LEMON BALM (*Melissa officinalis*), long praised by poets, is native to western Asia and has been cultivated since ancient times in southern Europe. It is found in gardens and semiwild in the eastern United States and California. It is also grown in Australia, Cuba, and Puerto Rico. An erect, bushy perennial (1-3 ft. high), it has somewhat hairy leaves (to 3 in. long), a delightful lemon fragrance, and aromatic, bitter taste. Fresh leaves

are put in fruit cups, salads, soft drinks, wine, and punch. Fresh or dried leaves are used to flavor soups, stews, meats, vegetables, egg dishes, sauces, dressings, and vinegar; also liqueurs such as Chartreuse and Benedictine. A weak brew makes a very pleasant tea. Balm oil has some commercial value in flavoring beverages, ice cream, candy, and baked goods, and is used in perfumes. Grown from seeds or cuttings, or by root division.

57.

MARYLAND
DITTANY

MARYLAND DITTANY, or **STONE MINT** (*Cunila origanoides,* syn. *C. mariana*), is native from southern New York to Florida and Texas. It is a wiry perennial herb (8-16 in. tall) with hairless leaves (¾-1½ in. long) dotted with oil glands. Flowers are white, pinkish, or rose-purple. The flavor of the plant is pleasantly mintlike, and it was dried and steeped for tea by the Indians and early settlers alike. Propagated by division.

BERGAMOT (*Monarda didyma*), also known as **RED BERGAMOT, BEE BALM, CRIMSON BEE BALM, FRAGRANT BALM, OSWEGO TEA,** and **INDIAN'S PLUME,** is native to the eastern United States from Maine to Georgia and cultivated in temperate regions of the New and Old Worlds. It is a thick-stemmed perennial herb (2-4 ft. tall) with thin, soft leaves (3-6 in. long) having a pungent, lemonlike aroma and bitter flavor. Young tips are used to garnish fruit salads and cool drinks and to flavor apple jelly. Fresh or dried leaves are useful for seasoning and frequently steeped for tea. Easily grown from seeds or by root division in wet, acid soil, preferably in shade.

BERGAMOT

WILD BERGAMOT, or HORSEMINT (*Monarda fistulosa*), grows wild across southern Canada and down through the midwest and western United States to New Mexico. It is a slender plant (2-5 ft. tall) with slightly downy, strong-smelling foliage (2¼-4 in. long). Flowers are usually lavender but there are several varieties, one with crimson, one with deep-purple, and one with flesh-colored flowers. Indians chewed the leaves and also added them as seasoning when cooking meat. The young shoots and the mature leaves are dried and steeped briefly for an aromatic tea. **LEMON BERGAMOT** (*M. citriodora*, syn. *M. pectinata*) is native to the southwestern United States. It is an annual, hairy herb (1-2 ft. tall) with leaves 1¼-3 in. long. Flowers are white or pink with purple dots. The entire plant is pinkish when very young. Hopi Indians boiled the leaves with wild game. Both of these species are grown from seeds or by root division in dry soil and full sun. *Monarda austromontana*, native to northern Mexico, is locally called oregano and commonly used for food seasoning. It is also steeped for tea, which is considered good for the stomach.

LEMON
BERGAMOT

COYOTE MINT (*Monardella villosa*, syn. *M. sheltonii*), also called **HORSEMINT** and **PENNYROYAL**, grows wild along the dry coastal ranges of southern California. It is an erect perennial herb (1-2 ft. high) with downy, resin-dotted leaves (½-1 in. long) and purple, pink, or white flowers. The plant is noted for its sweet, spicy aroma, and the slightly bitter leaves have been much used, fresh or dried, for tea. *M. macrantha*, a creeping species (2-12 in. high) has somewhat purplish leaves (¼-1 in. long) and showy flowers. Both species propagated by division, flourish in sandy soil.

VIRGINIA MOUNTAIN MINT, or **WILD BASIL** (*Pycnanthemum virginianum*, syn. *Koellia virginiana*), grows wild in North America from Quebec to North Dakota and south to Georgia and Oklahoma and is occasionally cultivated. It is a slightly hairy perennial herb (to 3½ ft.), the upper part bushy, the leaves (1-2½ in. long) firm and aromatic. The Indians used the buds and pleasingly fragrant flowers for seasoning soup and meat. Easily grown from seeds and appreciated as a border plant by flower gardeners, even though it is often overlooked by most herb growers.

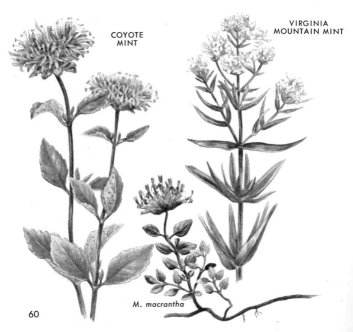

COYOTE MINT

VIRGINIA MOUNTAIN MINT

M. macrantha

AMERICAN
PENNYROYAL

AMERICAN PENNYROYAL (*Hedeoma pulegioides*), also known as **SQUAW MINT, STINKING BALM, TICKWEED,** and **MOSQUITO PLANT,** grows wild in North America from Quebec to Minnesota and south to Arkansas, and is sometimes cultivated. It is an unattractive, erect, branched herb (4-16 in. high) with nearly hairless leaves (½-1¼ in. long). The entire plant has a far-reaching fragrance and a pungent, mintlike flavor. It has served as a culinary flavoring; is more often steeped for tea taken as a home remedy. The essential oil is, like that of true pennyroyal, used in a small way in food manufacturing as a flavor for beverages, ice cream, candy, and baked goods. It is also combined with other strong natural scents, such as pine, to perfume industrial products. The crushed plant drives away fleas, ticks, and mosquitoes; the oil is used as an insect repellent. Grows readily from seeds, tends to run wild in dry sandy soil. *Hedeoma floribunda,* of northern Mexico, a low, spreading, hairy herb, with an abundance of pale lavender flowers, is locally called oregano or mapá, and is commonly used for seasoning and to make a tea taken to relieve indigestion.

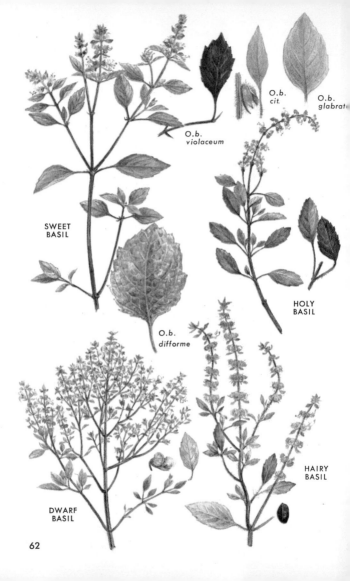

O.b.
violaceum

O.b.
cit.

O.b.
glabrat

SWEET
BASIL

O.b.
difforme

HOLY
BASIL

DWARF
BASIL

HAIRY
BASIL

SWEET BASIL (*Ocimum basilicum*), native to Central Asia, is grown in home gardens in all warm and temperate climates and cultivated commercially throughout Europe, Madagascar, and India. It is an erect annual herb (1-2 ft. high) with shiny leaves (to 1¼ in. long). Forma *citriodorum* is finely hairy, with white flowers, green calyxes, and a strong lemongrass odor. Forma *glabratum* is similar but less hairy and milder in aroma. Forma *violaceum*, with purple stems, flowers, leaves, and calyxes, has a strong aniselike odor. The curly variety *difforme*, called Italian basil, is most popular for home use. Fresh or dried young leaves and flowering tops are used to season soups, egg and vegetable dishes, seafood, poultry, meats, tomato sauce, and vinegar. Dried basil and oil of basil are important commercially for flavoring sauces, pickles, condiments, meat products, candy, and beverages. Basil oil is also used in perfumes, soaps, and dental preparations. In the Near East the seeds are eaten alone or added to bread dough. Their mucilaginous coating was formerly made into a tonic drink.
DWARF, or **BUSH, BASIL** (*O. basilicum* var. *minimum*), wild in India and widely cultivated, is smaller (6 in. to 1 ft.) and has yellowish-green or purplish leaves (to ¼ in. long). It has a spicy lemon odor and resinous, bitter taste, and is used for the same purposes as sweet basil. Both sweet and dwarf basil are grown from seeds and cuttings.

HOLY, or **SACRED, BASIL** (*Ocimum sanctum*) is native from western Asia to Australia and commonly cultivated in warm regions of the Old World. It is a perennial, bushy subshrub (1-2½ ft. high). Both the flower and calyx may be purple, or the flower may be purple or white and the calyx green. One form has purple leaves and stems. Holy basil is revered by Hindus and grown around temples. The tough stem bases are cut into beads for rosaries. The plant has a clove odor which is mildly intoxicating. Fresh leaves are added to salads and other cold dishes but are not used in cooking. The distilled oil may have a clove or anise odor; it is an effective antibiotic and insect repellent. Seeds are mucilaginous and used like those of sweet basil. Grown from seeds or cuttings, often in pots.

HAIRY, or **HOARY, BASIL** (*Ocimum americanum*, syn. *O. canum*) is found wild and cultivated from West Africa to India and the East Indies and has been introduced into North and South America. It is an erect annual herb (1-2 ft. tall) with downy leaves (to 2 in. long), usually camphorlike, sometimes thymelike in aroma. Mild young leaves are used in rice-and-curry dishes and to season seafood, meats, poultry stuffing, salads, soups, and sauces. The distilled oil, varying in odor from lemon to camphor, is used to scent soaps and other toilet products. The seed mucilage is used as a tonic. Grown from seeds, in dry soil.

EAST INDIAN BASIL (*Ocimum gratissimum*), also called **TREE,** or **SHRUBBY, BASIL,** is wild over most of India, Ceylon, and Oceania and cultivated in southern Europe and North Africa and in Brazil, where it has become naturalized. A semiwoody perennial shrub (3-8 ft. high), it has highly aromatic leaves (to 4 in. long), more or less hairy on the upper surface (especially when young) and gland-dotted beneath. Forma *caryophyllata* is strongly clove-scented. Forma *graveolens* is equally odorous but not clovelike and is distinguished by a purple tinge inside the lower lip of the flower. This form is used for culinary flavoring. Variety *suave*, with leaves velvety-hairy on both sides, has been much grown as an annual in herb gardens of France. The plant is avoided by mosquitoes and grown around homes for this practical reason.

TEA BUSH, or **FEVER PLANT** (*Ocimum viride*), of West Africa and cultivated in India, is a shrub (2-5 ft. tall). Its fragrant leaves (to 5 in. long), redolent of lemon thyme, are used in salads and for culinary seasoning, and steeped for tea, which is drunk as a beverage (with milk and sugar) and also as a fever remedy. The plant has many other medicinal uses, and its oil is an insect repellent.

CAMPHOR BASIL (*Ocimum kilimandscharicum*), a native of East Africa, cultivated in Africa and India, is a perennial shrub (5-10 ft. high) with leaves downy on both sides and strongly camphor-scented. This species, unlike its relatives, is valued primarily as a source of camphor, for which it has been grown commercially. Industrial uses are being sought for the decamphorized oil by-product.

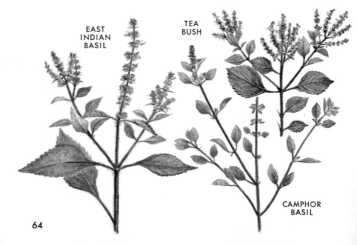

EAST INDIAN BASIL

TEA BUSH

CAMPHOR BASIL

ROSEMARY

ROSEMARY (*Rosmarinus officinalis*), a native of Mediterranean Europe and Asia Minor and widely cultivated, is a half-hardy, slow-growing, perennial shrub treated as an annual in cold climates. It is evergreen and usually erect (2-6 ft.), but one form is prostrate. The glossy leaves (¾-2 in. long) are dark green or striped with silver or gold above and downy-white below. Entire plant has a strong pine-nutmeg aroma and a warm, resinous, bitterish taste. Rosemary has a history of use reaching back 3,000 years, many romantic associations in legend and literature, and a symbolic role in European weddings and funerals. In Spain, baking ovens are scented with the herb. The downy and gray, tender young shoots and the milder flowers are used to garnish and flavor cold drinks, salads, soups, stews, pickles, and sauces for meat and fish. Mature leaves, fresh minced, or dried and powdered, are used domestically as seasoning for egg dishes, meats, seafood, poultry, soups, stews, vegetables, stuffings, baking-powder biscuits, and jam, and commercially in beverages, condiments, and meat products. Dried leaves have been much used in sweet sachets and for repelling moths. Rosemary tea is an old stomach and headache remedy. The essential oil distilled from the flowers alone, the leaves, or leaves and twigs is valued in perfumes and bath products. Grown by division or from cuttings, layers, or seeds, in full sun and dry soil. Serves as a compact hedge or low border in mild climates. May be cut back 3 times a year.

WILD MARJORAM (*Origanum vulgare*) is native to the British Isles, southern Europe, and western Asia, naturalized in the northeastern United States, and grown in most temperate regions. It is a hardy, straggly, erect or sprawling perennial (1-3 ft. high) with hairy, often purplish stems. The leaves (to 1½ in. long), golden-yellow in variety *aurea*, are slightly hairy, with a thyme-like odor and hot, pungent flavor. Flowers, usually purple, sometimes pink or white, are pleasantly fragrant, reminiscent of heliotrope, and much visited by honeybees. Fresh leaves and tender shoots are cooked as greens in India, and used to season soups, stuffings, and egg dishes, but are not popular. In the past, the plant was used in flavoring ale and beer. Dried leaves of the Mediterranean form (formerly set apart as *O. hirtum*), with copious oil glands, constitute most of the European "oregano" on the American market. Other closely related species, including *O. maru* (syn. *O. syriacum*), may also be sold as oregano. The dried plant has served as tea in England, has been blended with tobacco, and is often added to potpourri. In the past the flowering tops were the source of a purple dye. The acrid aromatic oil is used medicinally and in cosmetic and toilet products. Propagated by root division, cuttings, layers, or seeds. Needs full sun. **WINTER MARJORAM** (*O. heracleoticum*), from Greece, has identical uses. Propagated by division.

WILD
MARJORAM

WINTER
MARJORAM

SWEET MARJORAM (*Majorana hortensis*, syn. *Origanum majorana*), also called **GARDEN,** or **KNOTTED, MARJORAM,** from North Africa, is a perennial subshrub. It is erect (to 2 ft.), with purplish stems, wiry reddish branchlets, and velvety leaves (¾-1¼ in. long). The plant is pleasantly scented, with a somewhat camphorish taste when fresh but mellow and sweeter after drying. Sweet marjoram was cultivated by the ancient Egyptians and symbolized joy and honor in Greece and neighboring countries. It is still one of the favorites of herb gardeners. Tender sprigs are used as garnish and to flavor vinegar. Leaves and flowering tops, fresh or dried, are used to season salads, cooked vegetables, mushrooms, poultry, meats, seafood, omelets, stews, soups, sausages, stuffings, and sauces. Commercially, the dried plant is also important in baked goods and condiments. Seeds are aromatic and used in candy, beverages, condiments, and meat products. Oil distilled from leaves and flowering tops has a mint-nutmeg aroma, is used to flavor some foods and liqueurs; is more useful in perfumes, soaps, and hairdressings. Grown from seeds or, rarely, cuttings. **POT MARJORAM** (*M. onites*) of Mediterranean origin, is a hardier perennial (to 1 ft.) with strong thymelike aroma and flavor. It is used fresh or dried. Grown from cuttings, often in pots, indoors. Pot marjoram is prized in sachets and potpourri.

SWEET MARJORAM

POT MARJORAM

DITTANY OF CRETE, or **HOP MARJORAM** (*Amaracus dictamnus*, syn. *Origanum dictamnus*), from Crete and southern Greece, popular as a pot plant in cold climates, is a perennial, drooping subshrub (to 1 ft. high) with

DITTANY OF CRETE

SUMMER SAVORY

WINTER SAVORY

thick, woolly leaves (¾ in. long). It has been used to flavor salads and vermouth. Flowers are dried and steeped for tea. Dittany of Crete is grown from cuttings or seeds; it needs dry sandy soil and full sun.

SUMMER SAVORY (*Satureja hortensis*), of Mediterranean Europe and naturalized in the eastern United States, is one of the most popular herbs in cultivation. It is a bushy, spreading annual (to 1½ ft.) with densely hairy stems and sparse, soft leaves (½-1½ in. long) of sweet-resinous, peppery flavor. Fresh leaves and shoots used as garnish and in salads and rubbed on meat before cooking. Dried leaves and budding tips much used to season poultry, eggs, vegetables, sausages, soups, stews, gravy, stuffings, cakes, and puddings. Commercially, the herb is used in baked goods, condiments, and meat products. Grown from seeds in full sun.

WINTER SAVORY (*Satureja montana*), of Mediterranean Europe and North Africa and widely cultivated, is a hardy perennial with faintly downy stems (6 in.-2 ft. high) and stiff, slightly hairy, evergreen leaves (½-1 in. long). It is very attractive in full bloom and emits a spicy, resinous aroma. The flavor (except in winter) is stronger and sharper than that of summer savory, but young shoots and leaves are used in the same ways and also for flavoring liqueurs. Grown from seeds or cuttings, or by division or layers, in full sun.

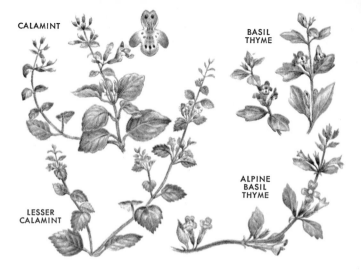

CALAMINT

BASIL THYME

ALPINE BASIL THYME

LESSER CALAMINT

CALAMINT (*Calamintha officinalis*), native from central Europe to the mountains of North Africa and western Asia, is an attractive, bushy, perennial herb (to 2 ft. high) with creeping rootstock and hairy leaves (to 1½ in. long). Of strong aromatic odor and pleasantly pungent flavor, it has been used to flavor roasts and stews; in Roman kitchens it was credited with removing the fetid odor and "gamey" taste of meat that had begun to spoil. **LESSER CALAMINT** (*C. nepeta*), of similar geographical range but at lower elevations, is a slightly smaller, grayish, hairy plant with leaves (to ¾ in. long) more deeply toothed, and lilac flowers on long stalks. It has a stronger odor and a pungent taste. Calamints are grown from seeds or cuttings.

BASIL THYME (*Acinos arvensis*, syns. *Satureja acinos, Calamintha arvensis*) is native from England and Scandinavia to the Caucasus and Asia Minor. It is an annual herb (to 8 in. high) with nearly hairless leaves (¼-⅝ in. long). Both the odor and flavor suggest thyme but are milder and pleasanter. In old English cookery, the flowering tops were used to season jugged hare. Sheep are partial to the plant, and it is said to impart an appealing flavor to the flesh of animals that eat it. **ALPINE BASIL THYME** (*A. alpinus*), which occurs wild in shady mountain regions of middle and southern Europe, is a perennial spreading herb (to 6 in. high) with roundish, slightly toothed leaves and pale violet flowers. Grown from seeds or cuttings.

SAGE, or **GARDEN SAGE** (*Salvia officinalis*), native to Mediterranean Europe, is widely distributed throughout temperate climates. It is a hardy, perennial, more or less sprawling subshrub (½-2 ft. high) with woolly, pebbled leaves (1-2 in. long). Some varieties, such as *albiflora* and *crispa*, have broad leaves; others, including *aurea*, *sturnina*, and *tricolor*, have foliage variegated with red, yellow, or white. Flowers are fragrant; usually purple or blue, sometimes white or pink. They are rich in nectar, and sage honey is in great demand in Europe because of its spicy flavor. In the days of sailing merchant ships, the Dutch carried cargoes of sage to China in exchange for tea. Sage (especially variety *tenuior*) is the leading culinary herb in the United States. It is grown commercially on the northwest coast and large quantities are imported, chiefly from Yugoslavia. Sage leaves have a strong scent and a warm, bitterish, slightly astringent taste. Fresh or dried, they are renowned as seasoning for stuffing, cheese, sausages, and pickles, and also for soups, stews, and cooked vegetables. Dried sage leaves are employed by food manufacturers in seasoning meats, baked goods, and beverages. They are used to flavor vermouth and various bitters and are a standard ingredient in spice mixtures. Sage tea has been much consumed as a beverage and is an old home remedy for minor ills. Sage extract and oil are important commercially in flavoring sauces, sausages, pickles, meat products, ice cream, candy, baked goods, chewing gum, condiments, and liqueurs. The oil is valued in perfumery and toilet preparations, especially those for men. It was an old custom to rub sage leaves on the teeth to clean them and benefit the gums. Sage is grown from seeds, cuttings, layers, or by division, in well-drained soil and full sun; should be cut back occasionally and replaced in 3 or 4 years when it becomes woody.

SAGE

PINEAPPLE SAGE (*Salvia rutilans*), an herb of unknown origin, but thought to be a horticultural form of the ornamental red sage (*S. splendens*), is a tender, bushy subshrub (2-4 ft. high) with soft, downy leaves having a distinctly pineapple fragrance. The flavor is milder than that of common sage. Young shoots are used to flavor cold drinks; fresh or dried leaves may be used in cookery like common sage and will not be so overwhelming. It is grown mostly from cuttings.

MEADOW SAGE, or **MEADOW CLARY** (*Salvia pratensis*), occurs wild from Scandinavia and the British Isles to Morocco and the Caucasus. It is a hardy perennial herb (1-3 ft. tall) with downy leaves (3-6 in. long). It usually has brilliant blue flowers, although many varieties in cultivation have flowers ranging from white to rose-red and dark-violet. Agreeable in odor, but with a pungent, bitter taste, this plant was formerly employed in flavoring beer and wine and was also used in England for tanning leather and as a source of an indelible brown dye.

APPLE SAGE (*Salvia pomifera*), indigenous to the Greek islands, is a woody shrub with showy inflorescences characterized by reddish or purple bracts. The bush is attacked by an insect which causes fruitlike, semitransparent galls (¾ in. wide) to develop on the branches. These agreeably flavored but slightly astringent growths, called sage apples, are candied and eaten

PINEAPPLE SAGE

MEADOW SAGE

APPLE SAGE

as sweetmeats. The leaves have a strong odor and flavor resembling those of lavender and common sage and are used to adulterate common sage for export.

CLARY

BLUEBEARD SAGE

CLARY, or **CLARY SAGE** (*Salvia sclarea*), of southern Europe and widely cultivated, is a biennial (2-3 ft. high) with thick stems coated with glistening hairs, and pebbled, hairy leaves (4-9 in. long). The thin upper floral leaves are white at the base and rose-tipped. The particularly handsome variety *turkestanica* has pinkish stems and white flowers tinged with pink. The flowers have an overpowering, far-reaching, spicy fragrance, with tones of pine and camphor. The foliage is of pronounced lavender-benzoin aroma. In former times, the young tender leaves were dipped in cream, fried and eaten with sugar-and-orange sauce, or dipped in beaten egg yolks and fried in butter. Chopped fine, they are added to soup and omelets and put into salads garnished with clary flowers. Clary imparts a muscatel flavor to wine and is grown in Germany especially for this purpose and for flavoring ale, beer, and liqueurs. A medicinal tea is made from the flowers. Essential oil distilled from the leaves and flowering tops is prized in perfumes, face powders, after-shave lotions, and soaps. Grown from seed; reseeds itself in dry sandy soil and full sun.

BLUEBEARD SAGE (*Salvia viridis*), ranging from southern Europe to Iran and sometimes cultivated, is the source of an essential oil that is used for flavoring wine and beer.

JOSEPH SAGE (*Salvia horminum*), which is also called **RED-TOPPED SAGE**, is a plant indigenous to southern Europe. It is an annual herb (to 1½ ft. high) with hairy leaves (1-2½ in. long). The upper floral leaves may be white (var. *alba*), red or purple (var. *purpurea*), or purplish-blue (vars. *violacea* and *vulgaris*). This was the principal sage cultivated by the ancient Greeks and Romans. They put the leaves and seeds in fermenting wine to spice it and increase its potency. The seeds served as a condiment and were also eaten fried with honey. In England, the leaves are added as a flavoring to cooked greens and soups. Joseph sage is grown easily from seeds and reseeds itself; is highly ornamental.

GREEK SAGE (*Salvia triloba*) grows abundantly on the lime-rich hills of Greece, southern Italy, and Sicily. It has heart-shaped leaves with two small leaflets at the base of each. The foliage, which is white beneath, is much woollier and stronger in odor than that of common sage, but it is gathered from the wild, and dried and mixed with the latter as an adulterant.

SPANISH SAGE (*Salvia lavandulifolia*), native to Spain and southeastern France, is mixed with common sage as an adulterant. Its essential oil is used commercially as a flavoring for ice cream, candy, baked goods, chewing gum, soft drinks, and alcoholic beverages.

JOSEPH SAGE

GREEK SAGE

SPANISH SAGE

73

THYME

THYME, or GARDEN THYME (*Thymus vulgaris*), native to southern Europe from Spain to Italy, is a perennial bushy herb (6-8 in. high) with wiry, white, hairy stems and tiny leaves (1/5-3/5 in. long), dotted with glistening oil glands on the upper surface and densely hairy on the underside. In ancient Rome and Greece, thyme was burned as incense and strewn on floors and graves. Old World beekeepers plant it around their hives, for the nectar is abundant and yields a fragrant, popular honey. The plant has a pungent odor defying description; some consider it to be minty and sagelike, others, a blend of camphor and spice. The taste is sharp, hot, and bitter and at the same time sweetish. Young shoots are used as garnish. The shoots, leaves, and flowering tops, fresh or dried, are commonly used for flavoring soups, gravies, stuffings, sausages, roasts, fish cakes, cheese, clam juice, pickles, and vinegar. In food manufacturing, dried thyme is most important as seasoning for soups, meat products, and baked goods. Thyme oil is employed mainly in chewing gum and condiments and to some extent in ice cream, candy, and alcoholic beverages. It is germicidal and commonly employed in mouthwash, gargles, dentifrices, cough syrups, lozenges, and other pharmaceutical preparations, as well as for scenting soaps. Thyme is usually propagated by division or cuttings, but grows readily from seeds; is replanted every 2-3 years.

AZORES THYME (*Thymus caespititius*, syn. *T. azoricus*, formerly included under *T. serpyllum*) is native to Spain, Portugal, the Azores, and Madeira. It is a subshrub with long, slender, woolly reclining branches that form humpy mats like moss. The narrow leaves (⅛ in. long) are gland-dotted on both surfaces, and have a soapy, tangerine odor. Fresh leaves are used for flavoring custards and are also often used as a substitute for, or in combination with, lemon thyme in general culinary seasoning. Grows readily from seeds and is accustomed to rocky situations.

CONEHEAD THYME, or **HEADED SAVORY** (*Thymus capitatus*, syn. *Coridothymus capitatus*), native to Mediterranean Europe and North Africa, is a subshrub (6 in. to 1 ft. high). Its branches are at first densely coated with white hairs. They become bare and spinelike with age. The stiff leaves (to ½ in. long) are dotted with oil glands, may be smooth or somewhat hairy, and are shed in dry, hot weather. The pink or white flowers are the source of the famed Hymettus honey of Greece. An essential oil, distilled from the dried plant, is commercially known as Spanish origanum oil. It is employed in the food industry mainly for flavoring baked goods, condiments, and meats, and, to a lesser extent, beverages, ice cream, and candy. Its most important use is in scenting soaps, colognes, after-shave lotions and other toiletries.

AZORES THYME

CONEHEAD THYME

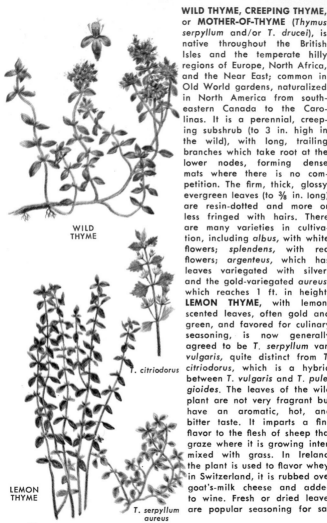

WILD THYME

LEMON THYME

T. citriodorus

T. serpyllum aureus

WILD THYME, CREEPING THYME, or **MOTHER-OF-THYME** (*Thymus serpyllum* and/or *T. drucei*), is native throughout the British Isles and the temperate hilly regions of Europe, North Africa, and the Near East; common in Old World gardens, naturalized in North America from southeastern Canada to the Carolinas. It is a perennial, creeping subshrub (to 3 in. high in the wild), with long, trailing branches which take root at the lower nodes, forming dense mats where there is no competition. The firm, thick, glossy evergreen leaves (to ⅜ in. long) are resin-dotted and more or less fringed with hairs. There are many varieties in cultivation, including *albus*, with white flowers; *splendens*, with red flowers; *argenteus*, which has leaves variegated with silver; and the gold-variegated *aureus*, which reaches 1 ft. in height. **LEMON THYME,** with lemon-scented leaves, often gold and green, and favored for culinary seasoning, is now generally agreed to be *T. serpyllum* var. *vulgaris*, quite distinct from *T. citriodorus*, which is a hybrid between *T. vulgaris* and *T. pulegioides*. The leaves of the wild plant are not very fragrant but have an aromatic, hot, and bitter taste. It imparts a fine flavor to the flesh of sheep that graze where it is growing intermixed with grass. In Ireland, the plant is used to flavor whey; in Switzerland, it is rubbed over goat's-milk cheese and added to wine. Fresh or dried leaves are popular seasoning for salads, sauces, stews, seafood, fish chowder, egg dishes, game and other meats, poultry, cooked vegetables, and vinegar. The flowers are dried and steeped for tea and also valued for sachets and potpourri. The essential oil is employed, mainly in Europe, in food flavoring, and in Benedictine, tobacco, dentifrices, soaps, and hairdressings. Grown easily from seeds, cuttings, or layers, or by division, lemon thyme is vigorous and needs to be trimmed to keep it within bounds. The variegated variety must be in full sun or it will revert to all green.

MASTIC THYME (*Thymus mastichina*), of Portugal and the Mediterranean coast of Spain and North Africa, is a perennial, hairy bush (6 in. to 1 ft. high) with leaves (to 3/5 in. long) which are whitish and gland-dotted when young, but become green as they grow older. The distilled oil, commercially called oil of wild marjoram, has a eucalyptus-camphor odor and pungent, bittersweet flavor. It is used extensively for flavoring meat sauces and soups.

OTHER THYME SPECIES. Many species and subspecies of thyme not ordinarily used for flavoring but fragrant and decorative are grown in rock gardens and as borders along paths or as carpetlike ground covers or filling between flagstones on terraces. *T. pulegioides* var. *chamaedrys* f. *kermesinus*, with crimson flowers, is one of the most showy.

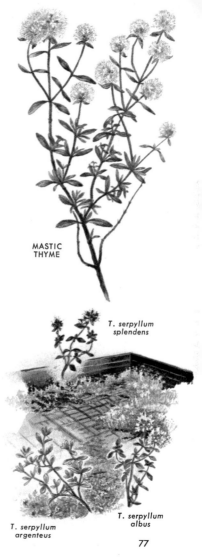

MASTIC THYME

T. serpyllum splendens

T. serpyllum albus

T. serpyllum argenteus

77

RUBIACEAE (Coffee Family)

CHEESE RENNET, also called **YELLOW BEDSTRAW** or **LADY'S BEDSTRAW** (*Galium verum*), is native from Iceland across the British Isles and Europe to the Himalayas, and naturalized in the eastern United States. It is a perennial herb with erect branches rising (6 in. to 3 ft.) from a creeping rootstock, and with hairy leaves (¼-1 in. long). Flowers smell of coumarin. The plant has no odor when fresh but is fragrant when dry and was a popular stuffing for mattresses in the past. Both the plant and flowers contain a milk-curdling enzyme and were commonly used to coagulate sheep's and goat's milks for cheese. Stems and leaves yield a yellow dye which served to color the cheese and also butter. Red dye from the roots was used for tinting wool. Cheese rennet has an acid, astringent, and bitter taste, and flowering tops are steeped to make an acid beverage. Usually propagated by root division, but may be grown from seeds. Suited to rock gardens if kept from spreading.

CLEAVERS, or GOOSEGRASS (*Galium aparine*), a weed in Europe and North America, is an annual, prickly herb formerly matted and used as a sieve. The dried plant has been steeped for tea, the seeds roasted as a coffee substitute.

CHEESE RENNET

CLEAVERS

SWEET WOODRUFF

SWEET WOODRUFF (*Asperula odorata*), native to Europe, Siberia, North Africa, and western Asia, is a perennial, creeping herb (6-12 in. high) with rough-edged leaves (1-1½ in. long). The flowers are fragrant but the plant is nearly odorless when fresh unless crushed; when dry it gives off the pleasant scent of coumarin. The flavor is astringent and somewhat bitter, and the leaves are not employed in cookery but rather as flavoring for beer and wine. In Germany, the fresh young shoots are steeped in Rhine wine, which is then called Maybowl or May wine and traditionally drunk on the 1st of May. Tinctures of sweet woodruff are used in some countries in pharmaceutical products but not in the United States where coumarin-containing flavorings are banned. In the perfume industry, sweet woodruff absolute is valued in creating "forest" tones. Powdered leaves enter into snuff, smelling salts, and potpourri. The dried plant was formerly hung and strewn in homes and churches for its fragrance and placed with stored clothing to repel insects. Propagated by root division or from seeds; makes a fast-growing ground cover or lush edging in semishade and moist soil.

GARDEN HELIOTROPE

VALERIANACEAE (Valerian Family)

GARDEN HELIOTROPE, or **COMMON VALERIAN** (*Valeriana officinalis*), also called **CAT'S VALERIAN** and **ST. GEORGE'S HERB**, grows wild in the British Isles and central Europe and across temperate Asia to Japan, and is widely cultivated as an ornamental and medicinal plant. It is a perennial (2-5 ft. tall), with compound leaves used to flavor tobacco. The flowers are spicily fragrant. The root, of strong, peculiar odor and warm, bitter, slightly acrid flavor, has long served in medicine as a sedative. Cats and rats are fond of it, and it is a bait for trapping wildcats and rodents. Root extract and essential oil are used commercially to simulate or enhance apple flavor, and to flavor ice cream, baked goods, condiments, root beer and other soft drinks, beer, liqueurs, and tobacco. In perfumery, the oil is valued in the blending of pine and balsam fragrances. Propagated by root division. Grows rapidly, forms suckers.

COMPOSITAE (Daisy Family)

YARROW, or **MILFOIL** (*Achillea millefolium*), is known by many other names, including **FIELD HOP** and **OLD MAN'S PEPPER**. It occurs wild in the British Isles, southern Europe, and western Asia, is naturalized in North America, Australia, and New Zealand, and is cultivated in Europe as a medicinal plant. It is a perennial herb (6 in. to 2 ft. high), with a creeping rootstock and hairy leaves (2-6 in. long). The flowers are typically white or pale lilac. The more ornamental varieties, *rubra* and *rosea*, with reddish blooms are preferred in flower gardens. The foliage has a mild scent and bitter, astringent taste; the flowers, stronger in odor, are bitterish and pungent. In the 17th century, yarrow gave zest to salads. The foliage and flowers were formerly added to fermenting beer to improve the taste and render it more potent. Essential oil from the flowering tops is used commercially for flavoring soft drinks and alcoholic beverages. Propagated by division or from seeds.

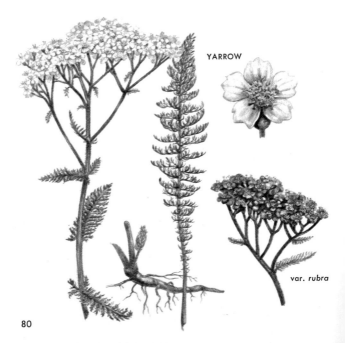

YARROW

var. *rubra*

CHAMOMILE, or ROMAN CHAMOMILE (*Anthemis nobilis*), is native to parts of the British Isles, western Europe, North Africa, and the Azores and cultivated in most mild climates. It is a perennial, hairy, creeping herb (4 in. to 1 ft. high) with finely downy, parsleylike leaves (to 2 in. long). The flowers are mild in odor but the plant has an applelike fragrance, for which reason it is called manzanilla in Spanish-speaking countries. Dried flowers are steeped for tea which many generations have appreciated as a pleasant beverage and which has been taken as a remedy for various ills. Essential oil and extract from the flowers are used in the food industry for flavoring ice cream, candy, baked goods, soft drinks, and alcoholic beverages. The oil has limited use in scenting tobacco and in perfumery and cosmetics. Chamomile rinse softens the hair. Propagated from seeds or cuttings, or by root division or layering of runners; needs full sun and dry soil; makes a durable path and compact mats between flagstones.

GERMAN, or HUNGARIAN, CHAMOMILE (*Matricaria chamomilla*), also called **SWEET FALSE CHAMOMILE**, is native to England, Wales, and southern Europe, and cultivated and naturalized in the eastern United States, Mexico, Cuba, and South America. It is an annual herb (to 2 ft.) with fine, lacy foliage. The plant has a mild pineapple aroma and bitter flavor. Dried flowering

CHAMOMILE

GERMAN CHAMOMILE

tops are steeped for aromatic tea consumed as a beverage and as a folk remedy. In the food industry, the essential oil plays a minor role, enhancing fruit flavors in ice cream, candy, baked goods, and chewing gum. It is more important in making liqueurs, such as Benedictine and D.O.M. The oil has been employed as a solvent in applying platinum to glass and porcelain. Both the dried flowers and the oil are substituted for those from true chamomile. The tincture is used as insect repellent. Grown from seeds in full sun and dry soil.

WORMWOOD (*Artemisia absinthium*), wild in England and from Lapland to Kashmir and commercially cultivated in many temperate regions, is a bushy, spreading perennial herb (1-4 ft. high) with ribbed stems and silky, hairy leaves (2-5 in. long). Entire plant has a strong odor which attracts dogs but repels fleas and other insects; it causes headache and nervousness in humans if inhaled excessively. The flavor is very bitter and astringent. It is one of the oldest known herbs in folk medicine, its use (to expel parasitic worms) traceable back to the ancient Egyptians. A weak infusion has the reputation of stimulating the appetite and improving the digestion. The Romans wove the plant into garlands, burned it as incense, and gave drinks of wormwood to victorious athletes to promote health and longevity. They put the herb in wine and indulged in wormwood potions before and after imbibing heavily. In the 17th century, the herb was a common seasoning for cakes. A preserve of wormwood, rose petals, ginger, and lemon was an early American remedy for seasickness. A coating of fresh wormwood during roasting is said to reduce the greasiness of goose. The tops have been added to hops in brewing, but the plant is most famed as the basis of the French aperitif absinthe, banned in 1915 for its narcotic effects, overindulgence resulting in insanity. The dried herb, its distilled oil (containing 50 percent thujone), and extract are still used in the food industry in flavoring ice cream, candy, and alcoholic beverages, including vermouth. The oil is an ingredient in rubbing liniments for muscular pains. Grown from seeds or cuttings. Dies back in winter.

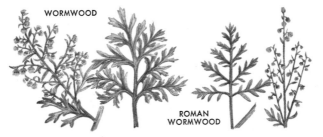

WORMWOOD

ROMAN WORMWOOD

ROMAN WORMWOOD (*Artemisia pontica*), also called **SMALL ABSINTHE**, is a native of central Europe and naturalized in the eastern United States. It is a perennial shrub (1½-4 ft. high) with downy leaves (½-2 in. long). The plant is milder in odor and flavor than common wormwood, but it is similarly a source of essential oil employed in vermouth and other wines. Grown from seeds or cuttings, or by root division.

MUGWORT, or **INDIAN WORM-WOOD** (*Artemisia vulgaris*), occurs wild in the British Isles, throughout Europe and temperate Asia, and in the northern United States; it is widely cultivated even in tropical countries. It is an erect perennial herb (2-8 ft. tall) with usually purplish-red ridged stems, and variable leaves (2-4 in. long), downy when young, green above and white-woolly beneath when mature. The ordinary type is not decorative but variety *lactiflora*, called **WHITE MUGWORT**, with white, fragrant flowers, and some variegated forms are grown as ornamentals. Mugwort was renowned in the past, from China to Scotland, as a magic plant or charm and was variously employed as a remedy. Fresh sprigs were added to beer and dried leaves and flowering tops were commonly steeped for tea in early England. The plant is pleasingly aromatic, with a sweetish, slightly bitter taste. Young shoots are cooked and eaten in Japan. Fresh leaves are sold for general culinary seasoning in the East Indies. Dried leaves are much used as seasoning for poultry stuffing. The distilled oil plays a minor role in food flavoring, is useful in perfumes and soaps. In the Orient, mugwort is an ingredient in joss sticks. Grown by division; spreads rapidly.

DAVANA (*Artemisia pallens*) is native and cultivated as a relatively new crop in India. An annual herb (to 2 ft.) with bluish-green, finely divided leaves, it

MUGWORT

DAVANA

has a delightful fragrance. Sprigs and flowers are worn, woven into wreaths, and used in garlands and bouquets for temples and festivals. The distilled oil is used commercially in ice cream, candy, baked goods, soft drinks, and chewing gum, as well as in perfumes. Grown from seeds which lose viability in a short time.

TARRAGON

TARRAGON, FRENCH TARRAGON, or ESTRAGON (*Artemisia dracunculus*), from southern Europe, Russia, and western Asia, is widely grown in cool and warm climates. It is an erect (to 2 ft. high) perennial (annual in the North) with smooth leaves (1-4 in. long). The plant has an aniselike odor and mildly pungent, licorice, somewhat camphorish flavor. Fresh leaves are commonly added to salads, pickles, and vinegar. Fresh or dried, tarragon is much used as seasoning for fish, meats, poultry, eggs, stews, soups, vegetables, sauces (especially Béarnaise and Tartar), and dressings. Dried tarragon is commercially important in seasoning canned meats and to some extent baked goods and condiments. Distilled "estragon oil," suggestive of anise, basil, and celery, is valued commercially for flavoring meats, baked goods, condiments, soft drinks, candy, and liqueurs. Propagated from cuttings or by root division; needs dry soil and sun or semishade. Dies back in winter.

SOUTHERNWOOD

SOUTHERNWOOD (*Artemisia abrotanum*), also called OLD MAN and LAD'S LOVE, of Mediterranean Europe and cultivated in warm climates, is a shrubby herb (2-5 ft.) with threadlike leaves (1-2½ in. long). It has a sweet, lemonlike fragrance but a pungent, bitter taste; its prime use has been in folk medicine. The young shoots are sometimes added to beer and, in Italy, used in cakes and confections. Propagated by division.

ELECAMPANE (*Inula helenium*) occurs wild from the British Isles to northern Asia and Japan and is naturalized in the eastern United States where it has been grown as a medicinal plant. It is a giant perennial herb (2-5 or even 10 ft. tall) with a hairy stem and soft leaves (8 in. to 2 ft. long), downy beneath. The young bitter leaves were formerly used as potherbs. The thick rootstock has a strong orris-and-camphor odor and was a medicinal and culinary favorite in ancient Greece and Rome and early England. Although bitter, it was used to flavor puddings and fish sauces, as well as beer, absinthe, and vermouth. It was popular candied, colored with cochineal and shaped into various forms, or mixed with dates and raisins. Dried and powdered, it was blended with honey and vinegar as a tonic. Essential oil is valued in perfumes. Grown from seeds or by root division in moist soil and full sun. Needs 3-4 ft. space between plants.

CANADA FLEABANE (*Erigeron canadensis*) is native to North America and a naturalized weed over most of the temperate world. It is an erect annual (to 3 ft.) with hairy leaves (1-4 in. long), of agreeable odor and bitter taste, which irritate the skin. It has had considerable use in medicine but not as a culinary herb. The essential oil, containing limonene, is used to some extent in commercial flavoring of candy, condiments, and soft drinks. Not cultivated.

ELECAMPANE

CANADA FLEABANE

POT
MARIGOLD

POT MARIGOLD, or CALENDULA
(*Calendula officinalis*), native to
southern Europe and eastern
Asia and universally grown as
an ornamental, is an annual,
hairy herb (1-2 ft. high) with
soft, more or less bristled leaves
(2-6 in. long). The showy flower
heads range in color from pale-
yellow to deep-orange. The pot
marigold appears often in classical literature, having been since
time immemorial favored in India, Egypt, Turkey, and many
parts of Europe as a symbolic,
healing, and culinary plant. For
kitchen use, single are preferred
to double forms. The flowers
have little taste raw but are
bitterish and savory when
cooked. Fresh chopped flowers
have been added to salads.
Dried flowers were commonly
used in early England and
France, Holland, and colonial
America for coloring and flavoring seafood, soups, game and
other meats, cheese, butter,
cakes, cookies, puddings, and
wine, as well as in medicinal
teas, syrups, conserves, and ointments. They serve as a substitute
for, or adulterant of, saffron.
Food manufacturers use the marigold in soft drinks, ice cream,
candy, and baked goods. To
make marigold buns, the ray
flowers (often miscalled petals)
are soaked in milk before blending with flour and other ingredients. In France the floral extract
enters into some subtle perfumes. People used to rub the
fresh flowers on bee and wasp
stings to relieve pain and swell-
ing. Grown from seeds in fairly
moist soil and full sun.

WILD MARIGOLD (*Tageta minuta*, syn. *T. glandulifera*), also called **STINKWEED** or **KHAKI WEED**, occurs wild from Peru and Brazil to Chile and Argentina, and is a naturalized weed in Africa, Australia, Hawaii, southern Europe, and the southeastern United States. It is an erect annual (6-10 ft. high) with feathery leaves (2-6 in. long) and emits a strong odor. In Africa it is grown near houses and hung in doorways to keep out flies and is a popular "insect-proof" mattress stuffing. The plant has a skin- and eye-irritating juice. Still, it has many uses in folk medicine. The leaves, applelike in odor when dried, are used for food seasoning in Chile and Peru and in the southern United States, where the plant is often grown as a culinary herb, especially for flavoring soups, meats, and vegetables. The essential oil (containing the possibly harmful tagetone) is used commercially to a limited extent in ice cream, candy, baked goods, gelatin desserts, and soft drinks. Distilleries in both the Old and New Worlds produce the oil and absolute for the perfume industry in which it is highly valued. Some years ago, Rhodesian and British scientists found that a root extract inhibits hatching of eelworms (nematodes), common destructive parasites, especially in warm climates and in greenhouses. Interplanting this marigold with ornamental, food, or other crops will protect their roots from nematode attack. Grows rapidly from seeds.

WILD
MARIGOLD

FRENCH
MARIGOLD

AZTEC
MARIGOLD

MARGARITA

FRENCH MARIGOLD (*Tagetes patula*) and **AZTEC MARIGOLD** (*T. erecta*), which is erroneously called African marigold, are both of Mexican origin. They are the most common species in flower gardens and universally cultivated. In parts of Asia, the East Indies, and Africa they have run wild. They are annual herbs (1-2 ft. high) with odorous leaves (2-3 in. long). Breeding has eliminated or modified the scent in many varieties. The flowers range in color from yellow to red (*T. patula*) or yellow to orange (*T. erecta*). They are revered in Mexico and India and adorn altars and cemeteries, and are used in religious ceremonies and festivals. These marigolds have had little use in Western cookery, but the leaves of *T. patula* serve as food seasoning in the Congo. In Africa and India the dried flowers are occasional adulterants of saffron and have been used to color butter, cheese, and textiles. A modern development is the use of marigold flowers in poultry feed to give the desired yellow color to the fat of chickens. Essential oil from both species is used in the food industry in the same way as that of wild marigold, but is not as important as the latter in perfume blending. Grown from seeds in dry soil and full sun.

MARGARITA (*Cosmos caudatus*), of Central America and the West Indies, is an annual (2½-6 ft. high) with feathery leaves (to 6 in. long) and deep-pink to dull-red flowers.

YELLOW COSMOS (*Cosmos sulphureus*), native from southern Mexico to Brazil, is also an annual (4-7 ft. high) with more finely divided leaves (4-18 in. long) and yellow to orange flowers. Yellow cosmos is more common than margarita as an ornamental. Leaves of both species have a turpentine odor when crushed and a strong, pungent flavor. When young and tender they are eaten raw, mixed with coconut, or cooked with other greens in the East Indies. Grown from seeds in dry soil and full sun.

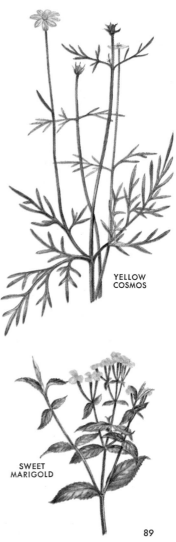

YELLOW
COSMOS

SWEET
MARIGOLD

SWEET MARIGOLD, SWEET MACE, or **ANISILLO** (*Tagetes lucida*), native to central and southern Mexico, is a somewhat woody perennial (1-1½ ft. high) with anise-scented leaves (2-4 in. long). It is one of the commonest herbs in Mexican folk medicine. The dried plant is frequently burned as incense. An anesthetic powder made from it was tossed in the faces of victims before they were burned alive by the Aztecs. This powder was also added to the Aztecs' *chocolatl*, a foaming beverage made from cocoa beans. In the 19th century, the plant was cultivated in English gardens and the leaves were in common use as a substitute for tarragon in seasoning soup. Bundles of the dried leaves and flowering tops are widely sold in Latin America for making an anise-flavored tea which is a popular and stimulating beverage. Grown from seeds; usually treated as an annual.

COSTMARY (*Chrysanthemum balsamita*) is also known as **ALECOST, SWEET MARY,** and **MINT**

COSTMARY

GERANIUM; as **MACE** in England, and as **BIBLE LEAF** (from use of a leaf as a bookmark in church). It is native to western Asia, has been widely cultivated in temperate climates, and is naturalized in southern Europe and the eastern and midwestern United States. A spreading perennial herb (2-6 ft. tall) with slightly downy leaves (2-10 in. long), it emits a sweet, lemon-mint-camphor odor and has a similar, but bitter flavor. In the 15th century the leaves were in demand for their fragrance and exported in quantity from Spain. Costmary was a popular culinary herb in ancient Egypt, Greece, and Rome and in common use in Spain, France, and Switzerland in the 9th century, and later in England. The young, tender leaves, plucked before blooming, were chopped and added to salads and sauces, put in stuffing for veal, and used in fermenting ale and beer. Leaves have been laid in cake pans to flavor cakes while baking, and also used to season game and other meats, poultry, and stews. The dried leaves have been frequently steeped for tea. Costmary seldom sets seeds. Grown by division and root cuttings. Does not bloom in shade. Fast growing, forming clumps. Dies back in winter.

CHRYSANTHEMUMS are important in Japanese cookery, for which special types have been developed. The flowers, fresh or dried, are pickled, or are boiled or fried and eaten with raw fish or in salads and soups.

CHRYSANTHEMUM

TANSY (*Tanacetum vulgare*), also called **BUTTON BITTERS**, grows wild from Britain and Scandinavia to Siberia and the Caucasus and is widely naturalized in North America and cultivated in central Europe and the midwestern United States. It is an erect perennial (2-3 ft. high) with a creeping root and feathery leaves (6-8 in. long) of strong balsam-camphor odor and pungent, bitter flavor. It taints the milk and butter of dairy cows. **FERN-LEAVED TANSY** (var. *crispum*) is an attractive ornamental. In Victorian England, tansy was renowned as a healing herb: tansy tea was taken as a tonic, although overdoses occasionally caused fatalities. Tansy leaves were rubbed on raw meat to protect it from flies and were added to ale. Bitter little egg-and-tansy cakes were eaten during Lent. Tansy-flavored omelets, "tansies" (puddings made of eggs, cream, bread, tansy, and other herbs), and tansy fritters were prominent dishes at feasts, as were apple tansies (fried apples with a sauce of eggs, cream, spinach juice, tansy, and rosewater). Tansy cake was a prize in handball games played by clergymen and parishioners at Easter. In Finland, clothing was formerly dyed green with tansy juices. Young tansy leaves, chopped fine, are today used sparingly in salads, egg dishes, stews, and cheese, and as seasoning for baked fish. The essential oil contains the toxic thujone; although it is not used as a food flavoring it is still used in liqueurs, especially

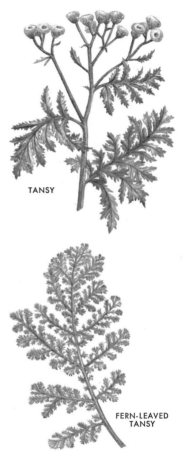

TANSY

FERN-LEAVED TANSY

Chartreuse. It has limited use in perfumery. Grown by division or from seeds; reseeds itself.

91

IMMORTELLE

FRAGRANT
GOLDENROD

IMMORTELLE, or **EVERLASTING** (*Helichrysum orientale*), native to southern Europe and Asia Minor, is a perennial subshrub (6-18 in. high) with narrow leaves (1-3 in. long), covered with loose down. *H. angustifolium,* of southern France and Italy, is a smaller plant (to 15 in.) with threadlike leaves (½-1½ in. long) covered with tight down. Both species are dried for decoration. Both are grown commercially in Yugoslavia, Italy, and France for the essential oil and extract, which are used to enhance fruit flavors in candy, ice cream, baked goods, soft drinks, and chewing gum. The oil is prized in perfume blending. **HOTTENTOT TEA** (*H. serpyllifolium*) was much used a century ago as a tea plant by Hottentots and Europeans in South Africa, but it has been suspected of causing ill effects.

FRAGRANT, or **SWEET, GOLDENROD** (*Solidago odora*) grows wild in the United States from New England to Texas and is cultivated in gardens. It is a perennial herb (2-5 ft. tall) with leaves (1½-4 in. long) minutely dotted with oil glands. When crushed, the leaves emit a pleasant anise odor. In pioneer days, the leaves were gathered, dried, and sold for making the popular and reputedly wholesome mountain tea. Dried flowers are also steeped for tea. The essential oil has been produced experimentally as a flavoring for candy and soft drinks. Grown from seeds in dry, sandy soil, and requires full sun.

92

DANDELION (*Taraxacum officinale*), native to Europe and eastern Asia, is a common weed in temperate climates and is sometimes cultivated. It is a perennial herb with a rosette of leaves (to 12 in. long) rising from a fleshy taproot. **RED-SEEDED DANDELION** (*T. laevigatum*, syn. *erythrospermum*), from Eurasia, is less common. The leaves of both species are bitter, but when young and tender are eaten in salads and cooked as greens. The root also is eaten raw or cooked and is often dried and roasted as a coffee substitute. Leaves and flowers are used to make wine. Extracts of the plants and roots are used commercially to flavor ice cream, candy, baked goods, and soft drinks. Grown from seeds.

SWEET HERB OF PARAGUAY (*Stevia rebaudiana*) is native to the mountains of Paraguay and the adjacent Mato Grosso region of Brazil. It is an annual herb (1-1½ ft. high) with leaves containing the compound stevioside, a substance 300 times sweeter than sugar. The natives grind the dried leaves for use as a sweetener or soak them in water and use the liquid in making preserves. Since the early 1900's there has been periodic interest in this plant as a nonnutritive, seemingly nontoxic sugar substitute. But production has proved too expensive. Indian women take a decoction of the plant as a contraceptive. Tests with laboratory rats have confirmed that it reduces fertility.

DANDELION

SWEET HERB
OF PARAGUAY

SPICES

Spices have played a romantic and dramatic role in history. The mention of spices conjures up visions of the mysterious Far East and caravans crossing Asian and African deserts. More important, the search for spices led to the discovery and exploration of the New World and the colonization of the tropics. Today, spices still exert a major influence on the world's economy.

Although the glamour of the spice trade is usually associated with the Orient, many of the leading spices are tropical American (vanilla, chili pepper, allspice, and sarsaparilla), African (myrrh, frankincense, kola nut, grains of paradise, and buchu), and European (saffron, myrtle, and labdanum). Eastern North America is the home of sassafras.

India today leads in production and export of spices, and the largest market for spices is the United States. In terms of quantity, pepper is the world leader, with more than 25,000 tons of black and white pepper consumed annually in the United States alone. The most costly spice is saffron, mainly from Spain, which has sold at $90 to $100 a pound!

Since about 1950, the spice industry has been growing steadily in Latin America. Most plantations are in Guatemala, Brazil, Argentina, and Mexico, but spices are also important crops in the West Indies.

Spices are usually imported whole, then distributed to processors who grind and package them, or produce essential oils, essences, and oleoresins for flavoring and perfumery. Nearly half the total spice supply goes to food manufacturers for use mainly in meat products, not only as flavoring but also for the antioxidizing action of spices on animal fats.

LICHENES (Lichen Class)

OAKMOSS is the trade name for the **STAG'S HORN**, or **RAGGED HOARY, LICHEN** (*Evernia prunastri*), a native of central and southern Europe and North Africa. It is an antler-shaped lichen, gray-green on top and white beneath, which grows in shaggy layers on oak, plum, and other trees. Another lichen, *E. furfuracea*, grows primarily on spruce and pine trees. These and other aromatic lichens are collected in quantity and were formerly exported to Egypt for flavoring bread. Their prime importance today is for distillation to produce extracts of great value in perfumes and for scenting soaps. In the food industry, oakmoss absolute is used mainly to flavor condiments. There is very limited use in baked goods and soft drinks.

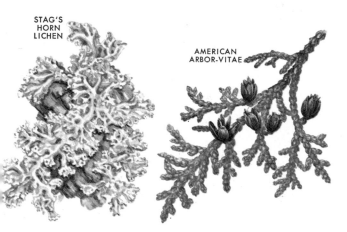

STAG'S HORN LICHEN

AMERICAN ARBOR-VITAE

CUPRESSACEAE (Cypress Family)

CEDAR LEAF OIL is derived from the **AMERICAN ARBOR-VITAE**, or **NORTHERN WHITE CEDAR** (*Thuja occidentalis*). Native from Quebec to Minnesota and south to Tennessee and widely cultivated, it is an evergreen shrub or tree (to 60 ft.) with many varieties. Leafy branchlets have been steeped for tea. More important, they are distilled for their essential oil which, after removal of the toxic thujone, is used commercially in flavoring meat products, baked goods, candy, and alcoholic beverages, as well as in perfumes, soaps, paints, and insecticides.

JUNIPER BERRIES are the fruits of the **COMMON JUNIPER** (*Juniperus communis*), of Europe, temperate Asia, North Africa, and North America. The juniper is a variable plant, ranging in size from a low, spreading shrub with stiff leaves (¼-½ in. long) to a 20-ft. tree. The berries are aromatic, with a sweet, pungent, turpentine flavor and bitter aftertaste. They are used as a pep- per substitute, and for flavoring sauerkraut; they are roasted to make mock coffee; are fermented with barley to make beer and brandy. Great quantities are gathered in southern Europe. Commercially, the dried berries and the oil distilled from them are used mainly to flavor gin, liqueurs, and cordials and also enter into soft drinks, condiments, and meat products. The oil is important in perfume.

COMMON JUNIPER

BALSAM FIR

PINEACEAE (Pine Family)

BALSAM FIR OIL is obtained from the **BALSAM FIR**, or **BALM OF GILEAD FIR** (*Abies balsamea*). Native from Newfoundland to Minnesota and West Virginia, the balsam fir is an evergreen tree (to 80 ft.) with highly aromatic foliage. Gummy, yellow resin, called Canada balsam, exudes from the trunk and has been sold for chewing, and as an adhesive for microscope lenses. An oleoresin derived from the resin and the essential oil distilled from the leaves and twigs are used to a small extent in flavoring candy, baked goods, ice cream, and beverages. They also enter into perfumes and household sprays.

SPRUCE OIL is obtained from four North American evergreens: **BLACK SPRUCE** (*Picea mariana*), which is wild from Labrador to Alaska and south to Wisconsin and Virginia, is usually 20-30 ft. tall, but may be much higher; **WHITE SPRUCE** (*Picea glauca*, syn. *P. alba*), also called **SKUNK**, or **CAT, SPRUCE**, because of its peculiar odor, is native from Labrador to northern New York and west to Montana and Alaska, and grows to 70 ft. in height; **CANADA HEMLOCK** (*Tsuga canadensis*), which ranges from Nova Scotia to Minnesota and south to Alabama, becomes 100 ft. tall; **WESTERN HEMLOCK** (*Tsuga heterophylla*), wild from Alaska to California and Idaho, attains a maximum height of 200 ft. Spruce oil, distilled from the leaves and twigs of these four trees, is used commercially to flavor chewing gum, ice cream, soft drinks, and candy. It is also used in perfumes, soaps and other toilet products, household sprays, and cleaning preparations. White and black spruce trees exude a gum that has been a popular substance for chewing. In the past the young twigs of the latter two trees—and the **RED SPRUCE** (*Picea rubra*)— were boiled with honey or molasses and fermented with yeast to produce the old-time favorite "spruce beer," which was consumed in great quantities. Leaves of the red spruce and Canada hemlock have frequently been steeped for tea by lumbers in Canada and the northern United States.

BLACK SPRUCE

WHITE SPRUCE

CANADA HEMLOCK

WESTERN HEMLOCK

RED SPRUCE

LILIACEAE (Lily Family)

SARSAPARILLA is derived mainly from two species of *Smilax*: *S. aristolochiaefolia*, of southern Mexico, Guatemala, and British Honduras, and *S. regelii*, native to British Honduras, Guatemala, and Honduras. Unlike many related greenbriers of the United States and elsewhere, which have thick, tuberous, starchy roots, these woody, spiny vines have long, slender, ropelike roots. Sarsaparilla roots were long famed as a remedy for venereal disease and are still utilized in pharmaceutical products. The extract has long been popular in root beer, and is used today in ice cream, candy, and baked goods.

S. aristolochiaefolia

SAFFRON CROCUS

IRIDACEAE (Iris Family)

SAFFRON is the product of the **SAFFRON CROCUS** (*Crocus sativus*), supposedly native to Asia Minor and much cultivated from Spain to the Far East. It is a perennial bulb producing, in late fall, lavender, red-purple, or white flowers, and later, slender leaves (1-1½ ft. tall). The stigmas of the flowers, separated and sun-dried, or sifted from the dried and beaten flowers, are orange-red, aromatic, pungent, and bitter, and constitute the spice widely used for flavoring and coloring rice, curries, meat products, breads, confectionery products, puddings, cheeses, butter, and liqueurs. The extract enters into condiments, ice cream, candy, baked goods, and soft drinks.

ZINGIBERACEAE (Ginger Family) is best known as the source of ginger, the most important rhizome (rootstock) in the spice trade. It embraces as well similar plants such as cardamom, of which the main products are the dried fruits and aromatic seeds. All members of this family are herbaceous plants but are never classed with herbs for horticultural or culinary purposes.

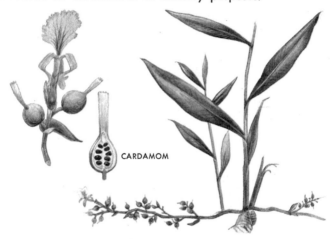

CARDAMOM

CARDAMOM (*Elettaria cardamomum*, syn. *Amomum cardamomum* L.) is native to India, Ceylon, and Malaysia and cultivated mainly in India and Guatemala. It forms clumps (5-18 ft. high) of long stalks with sheathing leaves (1-3 ft. long). Flowers and fruits are borne in long trailing sprays. Fruits range from nearly round to oblong, and are more or less ribbed; each contains 14-20 angled seeds coated with sweetish mucilage. They are harvested slightly unripe to avoid splitting, are dried in the sun or in kilns and sometimes bleached, and sold whole to conserve the aroma of the seeds. In India the fruits are chewed by people of the upper classes. The seeds, of sweet-balsam-eucalyptus odor and flavor, are ground for use in curry powder, condiments, pickles, meat products, especially sausages, and baked goods. Their essential oil is used similarly and also in alcoholic beverages, bitters, and candy. It is prized in perfume.

NEPAL CARDAMOM

BENGAL CARDAMOM

CAMBODIAN CARDAMOM

NEPAL, or **HILL, CARDAMOM** (*Amomum subulatum*) is grown in the wetlands bordering rivers in mountainous northern India and in neighboring Sikkim and Nepal. It is a perennial reaching 15-25 ft. in height. Flowers are borne in long, reclining sprays extending from the base of the plant. The fruits, containing sweet pulp and 40-50 camphorous seeds, are used locally mainly for making sweetmeats and are exported to the Near East as inexpensive substitutes for true cardamom. After the fruits mature, the plant dies back; new shoots come up from the rootstock. Propagation is usually by division. Plantations thrive for 25-100 years.

BENGAL CARDAMOM (*Amomum aromaticum*) occurs wild in northeast India and is cultivated from the Himalayas to North Vietnam. It is a plant (2-3 ft. high) with 2-2½-ft. leaves and hanging clusters of fruits. The fruits are chewed with betel nut, and the seeds used as seasoning for soups, meat, and fish.

CAMBODIAN CARDAMOM (*Amomum krervanh*), native to Cambodia and Thailand, is a plant (to 10 ft.) with leaves to 2 ft. long. The fruits contain 5-9 round seeds, are camphor-flavored, and used locally as spice in curries and cakes and sent to northern Europe for seasoning sausages, liqueurs, and especially bitters. They are exported to China where they are an important ingredient in prepared condiments.

TAVOY, or **BASTARD, CARDAMOM** (*Amomum xanthioides*), of Burma, Thailand, Laos, and Cambodia, produces seeds which are used in China to flavor liqueurs. These seeds have been exported to India and to London as substitutes for true cardamom, although they are smaller, stronger, and not so pleasant in odor and flavor.

JAVA CARDAMOM (*Amomum maximum*, syn. *A. dealbatum*) grows wild in moist teak forests in Java and is commonly cultivated. It is a robust plant (5-10 ft. high) with leaves (2-3 ft. long) that are agreeably fragrant when they are crushed. Young shoots and old leafstems of this plant are peeled and the inner portion, or heart, eaten raw. The young flower clusters and immature fruits are cooked with rice. The sour-sweet pulp around the seeds is enjoyed raw. The seeds themselves are used for seasoning.

ROUND, or **CLUSTER, CARDAMOM** (*Amomum compactum*, syns. *A. kepulaga* and *A. cardamomum* Willd.) is an aromatic plant (5-10 ft. high), native and commonly cultivated in Java. The leaves emit a strong turpentine odor when they are bruised. The young, pungent shoots are cooked and eaten with rice. The fruits have a sweet, turpentine aroma and flavor and are much used as food seasoning. They are popularly chewed to sweeten the breath and as a cold preventive. The seeds are used in cakes.

TAVOY
CARDAMOM

JAVA
CARDAMOM

ROUND
CARDAMOM

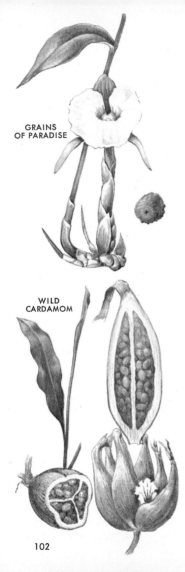

GRAINS
OF PARADISE

WILD
CARDAMOM

GRAINS OF PARADISE (*Aframomum melegueta*), also known as **GUINEA GRAINS, MELEGUETA PEPPER,** and **ALLIGATOR PEPPER,** is native to West Africa and cultivated in Surinam and Guyana. The plant forms clumps of stems (to 5 or 6 ft.), has leaves to 8 in. long, and solitary showy flowers. The fruits, ovate, and orange or red, are larger than cardamoms; they contain glossy brown conical seeds, which are aromatic, pungent, and camphorous. This is the leading spice of the Gold Coast and was the subject of lively trade with Europe as early as the 13th century, being used as pepper and for spicing wine and beer, a practice abolished by King George III. In India the seeds are used to flavor cordials and liqueurs. American food manufacturers use them in ice cream, candy, and soft drinks. Previously, the spice was believed to be derived also from a similar West African plant, *A. granum-paradisi*, used locally.

WILD, or **MADAGASCAR, CARDAMOM** (*Aframomum angustifolium*), native to East Africa and Madagascar, has stems up to 12 ft. with leaves to 15 in. and flowers in clusters of 3 or 4. Both the stems and leaves emit a spicy aroma when crushed. The fruits contain agreeable acid pulp as well as many small brown seeds and are eaten fresh. Separated and dried, the seeds are used like pepper for seasoning. In the Near East they are added to coffee and claimed to be an aphrodisiac.

GINGER (*Zingiber officinale*), presumably native to Oceania and cultivated in all warm countries, forms clumps of stems (to 4 ft. high) with leaves to 1 ft. long. Flower spike (rare in some climates) is on a separate stalk emerging from the creeping, pungent rhizome. Ginger is one of the oldest known and most widely consumed spices. Very young rhizomes (green ginger) are peeled and eaten raw or cooked in syrup, as a sweetmeat, and are often candied. Fresh ginger is important in curries and chutneys. Older roots are scalded and scraped (white ginger) or merely scalded (black ginger) and coated with lime for the market. Chunks add zest to preserved fruits and pickles. Ground ginger is used in curry powder. Essential oil, distilled from fresh rhizomes, as well as ginger oleoresin and extract are extensively employed in baked goods, meat products, sauces, condiments, ice cream, candy, liqueurs, and soft drinks.

WILD, or **BITTER**, **GINGER** (*Zingiber zerumbet*, of which so-called *Z. aromatica* is a variety) is of doubtful origin but abundant in the wild from Southeast Asia and the East Indies to Hawaii. It attains 2 ft. with leaves 4-8 in. long, and produces flowers on a separate stalk. The inflorescence is rich in mucilaginous juice that relieves thirst. Young leaves and shoots are cooked in Malaysia, and leaves are used to flavor meat in Hawaii. Tender tips of young rhizomes are eaten raw in Java and Madagascar.

GINGER

WILD GINGER

103

JAPANESE

JAPANESE, or MIOGA, GINGER (*Zingiber mioga*) occurs wild and cultivated throughout Japan and is also grown in Hawaii. It is a deciduous plant (1½-3 ft. high) with thin leaves (to 1 ft. long) and separate short-stalked flower spikes, appearing continuously from summer through fall. Since the rhizome is inedible, this ginger should really be classified as an herb. The aromatic, pungent young leaves and long leaf bases, and the immature inflorescence, chopped fine, are used to give zest to soups, raw or fried fish, and soybean curd. Inflorescence is also pickled.

RESURRECTION LILY is a name applied to plants of the genus *Kaempferia*, three species of which, native to southern Asia and Indonesia, furnish spice. *K. galanga* is a low plant with 2 or 3 horizontal leaves (3-5 in. long) and a tuberous rhizome, camphorlike in odor and of aromatic, bitter taste. *K. rotunda*, with erect, elongated leaves (to 1½ ft.) has a nearly round rhizome with small auxiliary tubers. *K. pandurata* (recently transferred to the genus *Boesenbergia*) has 3 or 4 erect leaves (to 10 in. long on 1-ft. stalks) and long, tapering rhizomes. Young leaves, shoots, and tender rhizomes are eaten raw, used for seasoning, or steamed as a savory side dish. Rhizomes are also pickled. Powdered rhizome of *K. galanga* is sometimes substituted for turmeric in curry powder; it is also used for scenting clothes and cosmetics.

K. galanga

K. rotunda

GALANGAL, or **GREATER GAL-ANGAL** (*Alpinia galanga*), wild and cultivated from western India to Indonesia, grows to 7 ft. with fragrant leaves to 18 in. long. **LESSER GALANGAL** (*A. officinarum*), native to China and cultivated in Japan and Thailand, is smaller (to 5 ft.), with narrow leaves (to 12 in. long). Both have aromatic, pungent, bitter rootstocks which, when young and tender, are diced and added to Indonesian dishes. The extract and essential oil from both species are used mainly to flavor liqueurs such as Chartreuse, Angostura and other bitters, and soft drinks.

TURMERIC, or **INDIAN SAFFRON** (*Curcuma longa*, syn. *C. domestica*), is native to southern Asia and extensively planted in the tropics. The plant reaches 2-5 ft., and has 1-1½ in. leaves; a flower spike, on the same stalk, never develops seeds. The clustered, pungent, bitter rhizomes are rich in yellow-to-orange pigment, used as paint and as a dye. Young shoots and tips of rhizomes are eaten raw. Leaves wrapped around fish flavor it during cooking. Mature rhizomes are cured (by cooking and sun-drying), polished, and sometimes further treated and tinted for market. Powdered turmeric is an essential part of curry powder and prized for coloring and seasoning fish, poultry, meats, gravies, and rice. Commercially the powder, the extract, and oleoresin are utilized in soups, meat products, pickles, and condiments.

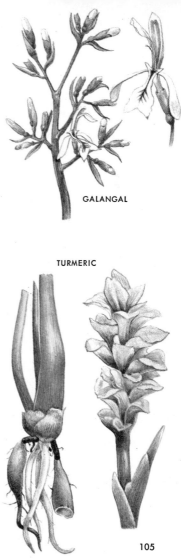

GALANGAL

TURMERIC

ZEDOARY (*Curcuma zedoaria*) is native to northeast India and cultivated throughout southern Asia and the East Indies. The plant (reaching 5-10 ft. in height) has purple-veined leaves (10 in.-2 ft. long) and flower spikes on separate stalks. The tender heart of the stems is eaten raw or cooked, and the leaves, resembling lemongrass in flavor, are cooked with fish as seasoning. Slices of the raw young rhizomes are added to salads. Mature rhizomes are large, gingerlike in odor, pungent and camphorous in flavor. They are rich in starch, which is extracted, debittered by repeated washing, and used like arrowroot as food for infants and invalids, and also made into confectionery. As a spice, zedo-ary is too musky for curries and is regarded as inferior to ginger. It is used outside the United States in Chartreuselike liqueurs and in bitters. In the American food industry, zedoary is employed only in soft drinks. *C. mangga*, with purple-tinted leaves, formerly treated as distinct, is now classed as a form of *C. zedoaria*. Common, wild, and cultivated in Java, it has a main, rounded rhizome (hairy and with an unripe-mango odor) and many slender side rhizomes. Young shoots and tender tips of the pungent rhizomes are eaten raw or cooked. Flower clusters are steamed and eaten with rice. **MANGO GINGER** (*C. amada*), of India, has a mild, mango-scented rhizome which can be candied or pickled.

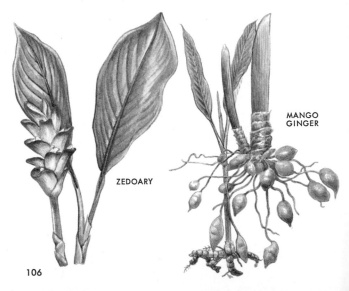

MANGO GINGER

ZEDOARY

ORCHIDACEAE (Orchid Family)

VANILLA is the product primarily of *Vanilla planifolia* (syn. *V. fragrans*), believed native from southeastern Mexico to Bolivia. This plant is a terrestrial climbing orchid with a zigzag stem, rubbery leaves (to 10 in. long), artificially pollinated flowers that last only one day, and clusters of seedpods—"vanilla beans" (to 1 ft. long). The pods are picked slightly unripe and cured by alternate drying and sweating for 2 weeks or more to develop odor and flavor. The Aztecs mixed chopped vanilla beans with chocolate and Europeans were quick to adopt this flavoring material. Today it outranks any other in domestic and commercial food enhancement. Vanilla beans, extract, and resinoid are used mainly in ice cream, baked goods, syrups, icings, and candy; also in puddings, soft drinks, liqueurs, and tobacco. **TAHITI VANILLA** (*V. tahitensis*) is a slenderer vine with short pods (to 6 in. long), red-brown when cured. Although inferior to *V. planifolia*, this is the commercial vanilla of Tahiti and Hawaii. **WEST INDIAN VANILLA** (*V. pompona*), native from Mexico to Trinidad, produces a short, thick pod called vanillon, formerly of importance but less fragrant than true vanilla. It is used mainly in liquors, tobacco, soaps, and perfumes. The plant has traits useful in hybridizing.

VANILLA

WEST INDIAN VANILLA

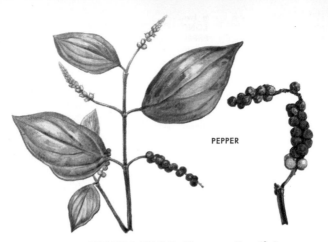

PEPPER

PIPERACEAE (Pepper Family)

PEPPER, or **BLACK PEPPER** (*Piper nigrum*), believed indigenous to the Malabar Coast of India, is of ancient culture in the Orient and deeply woven into the romance of the great spice trade of old. It has been grown extensively in Indonesia, for less than 500 years in Africa, and has seen only a quarter century as a commercial crop in the Western Hemisphere. The plant is a slender vine, with aerial roots, glossy leaves (4-6 in. long), and spikes of small flowers followed by pungent fruits ("peppercorns"), which turn from green to red and then black. Picked when slightly unripe and most pungent, the fruit clusters are trampled to detach the berries; these are heaped until they turn black and are then sun- or oven-dried. To produce

the milder **WHITE PEPPER**, the berries are picked ripe and soaked for a week to soften and remove the skins. The cleaned seeds are then dried. Ground pepper, usually a blend of black and white, is a familiar table seasoning and indispensable in cookery throughout much of the world. In food manufacturing, black and white peppercorns, whole or ground, are of major importance in soups, meats, baked goods, and pickles. White pepper is more useful in beverages. A pungent black pepper oleoresin is much used in baked goods and in sausages, pickles, condiments, and other highly seasoned products. Nonpungent black pepper oil is used with other flavorings mainly in sauces, dressings, vinegar, and canned meats.

LONG PEPPER comes from two plant sources: **INDIAN LONG PEPPER**, or **JABORANDI PEPPER** (*Piper longum*), is native to northeastern and southern India, Ceylon, and southeastern Asia; **JAVANESE LONG PEPPER** (*P. retrofractum*, syn. *P. officinarum*) is native from Malabar and East Bengal through Southeast Asia, Indonesia, and the Philippines. Both are subshrubs of climbing or trailing habit, with variable leaves (to 6 in. long). Trained to stakes and pruned, they bear a continuous supply of fruits tightly packed in spikes. The spikes of ripe, red berries are harvested and dried whole, turning slate gray. The Javanese is the more pungent of the two (even hotter than black pepper). Both are popular in the Orient in curries and pickles and are much used in Europe for home pickling, and sometimes are adulterants of black pepper.

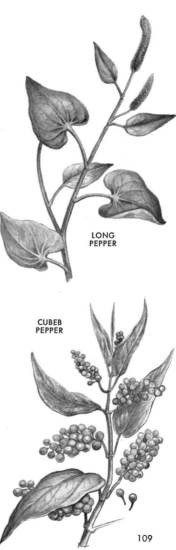

LONG PEPPER

CUBEB PEPPER

CUBEB, or **TAILED, PEPPER** (*Piper cubeba*), native to the East Indies and much grown in the Orient and Nigeria, may be vinelike or treelike with leathery leaves (3-6 in. long). The fruits, larger than black pepper, are orange when ripe but picked green with each tiny stalk attached. When dried, they are gray-brown or black with strong, spicy odor and aromatic, bitter, acrid flavor. In medieval Europe, cubebs were in demand as seasoning and for medicinal use. Today, the oleoresin enters into pickles, meat sauces, bitters, and tobacco. The essential oil is useful in perfumes and soaps.

WEST AFRICAN BLACK PEPPER (*Piper guineense*), also called **ASHANTI, BUSH,** or **BENIN PEPPER,** commonly found wild in forests of west tropical Africa, is a climbing shrub (to 40 ft.) with aromatic leaves. Fruits of this shrub, borne in loose clusters, are red or red-brown when ripe, black when dried. Milder than black pepper, they are much used, fresh or dried, to season soup, rice, and other foods. Leaves also put in soup.

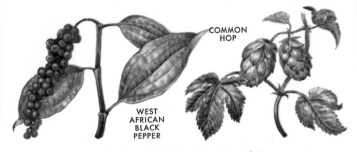

COMMON HOP

WEST AFRICAN BLACK PEPPER

MORACEAE (Fig Family)

HOPS are obtained from the **COMMON HOP** (*Humulus lupulus*), native in temperate Europe and Asia and in North America (sometimes distinguished as *H. americanus*) from Nova Scotia to Manitoba and south to Arizona and North Carolina. Extensive cultivation is carried on in central Europe and the northwestern and eastern United States. The plant is a twining perennial vine (to 30 ft.) with rough leaves having up to 11 lobes. Yellowish male flowers are borne in catkins (2-6 in. long); the female flowers are shielded by bracts forming soft "cones" in which the seeds develop (except in the new seedless varieties). At the base, the cones bear yellow glands containing the bitter lupulin, or "hop meal." This can be sifted as a yellow powder from the dried, beaten cones, or "hops." The ancient Greeks consumed only the young shoots of the vine, which are still eaten in salads or soup. Hops have served as a flavoring and preservative for beer since the 8th century. The hops are usually kiln dried, cured, and added to the boiling grain mixture into which they release their bitter and antiseptic properties. The distilled hop oil and hop extract are being used instead of hops by some brewers. Hop absolute and oleoresin are useful for other flavoring purposes, as in ginger ale and other soft drinks, spice mixtures, and sauces, and for enhancing apple, pineapple, and citrus flavors in food products.

CARYOPHYLLACEAE (Pink Family)

CLOVES are produced by the **CLOVE TREE** (*Syzygium aromaticum*, syn. *Eugenia caryophyllata*), indigenous to the Moluccas (the "Spice Islands") and cultivated mainly in Madagascar, the Comoro Islands, Tanzania, and Java. The tree is handsome (to 30 ft.) with aromatic leaves (to 5 in. long) and fragrant flowers. The unopened flower buds were prized by the Chinese in the 3rd century B.C. Cloves were popular in Europe by A.D. 700, and extensive exploration in search of this spice was begun by the Portuguese in 1600. Spicy, warm, whole or ground cloves are commonly used at home and commercially to season ham, sausages and other meats, baked apples, mincemeat pies, preserves, and pickles. Half the world supply is consumed in Indonesia, where the cloves are mixed with tobacco to make kretek cigarettes. Clove oil and extract are important in meat products, condiments, spiced fruits, candy, chewing gum, and liquors. Milder oil distilled from the leaves is much used to flavor meats; it is also valued in perfumes and soaps.

CLOVE
TREE

CLOVES

111

RANUNCULACEAE (Buttercup Family)

BLACK CUMIN (*Nigella sativa*), also known as **BLACK CARA-WAY**, **FENNEL FLOWER**, and **NUTMEG FLOWER**, is native from Greece and North Africa to northeastern India, and commonly cultivated in this region and in France and Germany. It is an annual (to 2 ft. high) with leaves to 2 in. long and 5-lobed fruits containing black, pungent seeds which emit a lemon-carrot odor when crushed. Referred to as "fitches" by the Prophet Isaiah in 725 B.C., the seeds preceded black pepper as spice in the Near East. They are sprinkled on a fine cakelike bread and extensively used for flavoring curries and other foods. Quantities are exported to Malaysia for medicinal purposes, and they are stored with clothing to repel insects. Essential oil of *N. damascena*, **LOVE-IN-A-MIST**, is valued in perfume and lipstick.

BLACK CUMIN

STAR ANISE

ILLICIACEAE (Illicium Family)

STAR ANISE, CHINESE ANISE, or **BADIAN** (*Illicium verum*), wild and cultivated in the warm parts of Southeast Asia, is a slender tree (to 45 ft.) with evergreen leaves (to 6 in. long), white to red flowers, and an 8-pointed fruit with (normally) a seed in each point. The sweet, aromatic fruit, which is picked unripe, is chewed after meals to aid digestion and sweeten the breath. In the Orient, star anise is a common flavoring for curries, confectionery, and pickles. The distilled oil is important in baked goods, candy, ice cream, and soft drinks; it is also used in anisette and other liqueurs. The Japanese *I. anisatum* is toxic.

ANNONACEAE (Custard Apple Family)

ETHIOPIAN PEPPER (*Xylopia aethiopica*), also called **GUINEA PEPPER, NEGRO PEPPER,** and **SPICE TREE**, native to west tropical Africa, is a stately tree (to 60 ft.) with aromatic bark, leathery leaves (to 8 in. long), and fragrant flowers. The fruit consists of clustered, podlike fingers (2½ in. long), each of which contains a half-dozen small, black seeds. The peppery fruits and seeds were formerly exported to Europe as spice, but have been replaced by black pepper. Locally, the fruits are dried, powdered, and used in coffee, palm wine, and various dishes, and often put in water to "purify" it. Other *Xylopia* species are similar. In the Belgian Congo, the fruits of *X. parviflora* are popular seasoning, as are those of *X. frutescens* in northern South America, and *X. carminativa* (syn. *X. sericea*) and *X. grandiflora* in Brazil.

YLANG-YLANG, or **ILANG-ILANG** (*Canaga odorata*), occurs wild from Burma to Queensland and is cultivated commercially in the Comoro Islands, northwestern Madagascar, and, to a lesser extent on islands in the Pacific and the West Indies. The tree (60-80 or even 120 ft.) is esteemed in all warm regions as an ornamental. It has drooping branches, evergreen leaves (5-8 in. long), richly scented flowers, and inedible fruits. Essential oil distilled from the flowers (usually picked at night when they are most fragrant) is regarded as the "Queen of Perfumes." It is extensively used in fine scents, face powder, and various other cosmetics. It has a little-known role in commercial fruit flavors (especially peach and apricot) for candy, icings, and baked goods, and also enters into soft drinks and chewing gum.

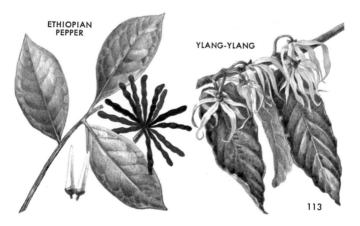

ETHIOPIAN PEPPER

YLANG-YLANG

CALABASH, or **CALABAR, NUT-MEG** (*Monodora myristica*), is native to west tropical Africa. The first specimen described was growing in Jamaica from seed brought by slaves and was given the misleading name Jamaica nutmeg. It is a deciduous tree (to 80 ft.) with smooth leaves (to 2 ft. long), showy, pleasantly scented flowers, and woody fruit (6-7 in. wide) containing fragrant pulp and spicy 1-in. seeds resembling true nutmeg in flavor. The dried seeds are sold throughout much of Africa for seasoning soups and other foods; they are also used in snuff, are made into necklaces, and are valued in local medicine. A variety (often called *M. grandiflora*) with colorful leaves and very large flowers is esteemed as an ornamental tree in botanical gardens.

CALABASH
NUTMEG

STRIPED CALABASH NUTMEG
(*Monodora tenuifolia*), native on
the African coast from Senegal
to Nigeria, is a shrub or tree (to
50 ft.) with striped bark, deciduous leaves (to 8 in. long),
sweet-scented blossoms, and
smooth fruits (to 4 in. long), each
containing over 40 aromatic
brown seeds (¾ in. long) much
used locally for seasoning.

YELLOW-FLOWERED NUTMEG
(*Monodora brevipes*) of Liberia
and southern Nigeria is a shrub
or tree (to 60 ft.) with deciduous
leaves (to 12 in. long), handsome flowers, and ribbed fruit
(to 3 in. wide). The aromatic
seeds are dried and used, often
in combination with Ethiopian
pepper, to flavor soups and
other foods.

ANGOLA CALABASH NUTMEG
(*Monodora crispata*, syn. *M. an-
golensis* in part), ranging from
Sierra Leone to the Cameroons,
is a climbing shrub or tree (12-
30 ft.) with 6-in. leaves, pretty
and highly fragrant flowers, and
aromatic seeds used like nutmeg.

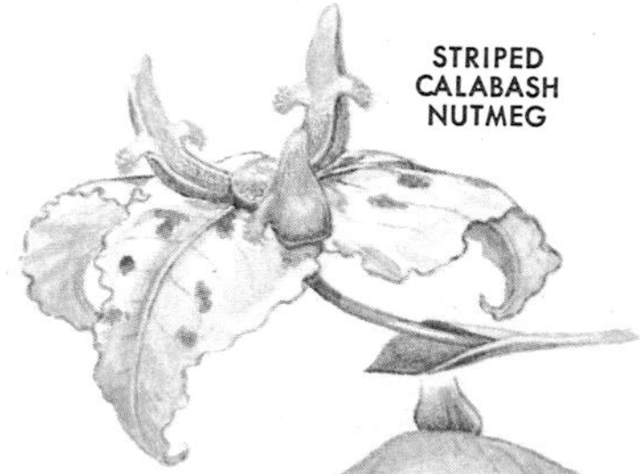

STRIPED
CALABASH
NUTMEG

YELLOW-FLOWERED
NUTMEG

ANGOLA
CALABASH
NUTMEG

115

MYRISTICACEAE (Nutmeg Family)

NUTMEG and **MACE** have been the objects of secret trading, monopolies, and strife. They are products of *Myristica fragrans*, a handsome tree (20-60 ft. high) native to the Moluccas and cultivated mainly in Indonesia and Grenada. The tree has evergreen, aromatic leaves (2-5 in. long) and a year-round crop of peachlike but tough, dry fruit. When ripe, the fruit splits open, revealing the large seed (nutmeg) partly clasped by a fleshy red network (mace). After the "husk" is removed, the mace is taken off and dried. One pound of mace is obtained from 400 pounds of nutmegs. Mace is powdered for home use in soups, sauces, and cakes. It is mildly nutmeglike in flavor and of great commercial importance as a seasoning in meat products, baked goods (including doughnuts), and soft drinks. Mace oleoresin is employed similarly and in pickles. The essential oil is used primarily to flavor candy and chewing gum. Powdered mace, sprinkled on cooked cabbage, masks the sulfide odor. The nutmeg itself is dried, shelled, and the kernel is usually limed and sold whole or ground. A sprinkling of nutmeg adds flavor to homemade custards and other puddings, eggnog, and pies. In

red MACE
surrounds NUTMEG

*Myristica
fragrans*

the food industry, nutmeg is primarily used in baked goods, ice cream, meat products, and soft drinks. Nutmeg oil is used mainly in chewing gum. Nutmeg fat ("butter") is used in perfumes, soaps, and candles. In quantity, both nutmeg and mace are toxic.

PAPUA, or **MACASSAR, NUTMEG** and **MACE** are derived from *Myristica argentea,* a tree of Macassar and New Guinea, with fruit longer and narrower than that of *M. fragrans.* The orange-colored mace is not in the form of a network but in 4 broad strips united at base and apex. Both the mace and the relatively smooth, reddish-brown seed kernel (to 1½ in. long) are less aromatic and milder in flavor than true mace and nutmeg. There is little market for these products except for local medicinal purposes and adulteration of mace and nutmeg.

BOMBAY, MALABAR, or **FALSE, NUTMEG,** and **BOMBAY MACE** are spices produced by *Myristica malabarica,* a tree native to the Malabar coast of India. The furry fruit (2½-3 in. long) and seed are larger than those of true nutmeg. The reddish-yellow, nearly cylindrical mace and the kernel have little aroma and flavor. Nevertheless, both have been frequently used to adulterate the true spices. Of value in its own right is the resin extracted from the seed, which serves as an antioxidant, preventing rancidity in edible fats and oils.

PAPUA NUTMEG

BOMBAY NUTMEG

MALE NUTMEG

MALE NUTMEG (*Myristica fatua*), native to the Moluccas and cultivated in Malaya, is a tree (to 60 ft.) with ovoid fruit (2-3 in. long) having a large seed clasped by a red, macelike aril. This species has been reported as yielding condiments, but neither the kernel nor the aril is more than faintly aromatic. The fat of the kernel is used to adulterate cocoa butter.

LAURACEAE (Laurel Family)

CINNAMON, or **CEYLON CINNAMON** (*Cinnamomum zeylanicum*), grows wild in western India and in Ceylon, which is also the center of cultivation. It is an evergreen tree (20-60 ft. high) with stiff, glossy leaves (to 7 in. long) of spicy odor and varying from sweet to pungent or bitter in flavor. Young trees are pruned to induce new shoots from which the bark is cut off in strips, bundled, and allowed to ferment; then the outer layer is scraped off and the bark rolled into "quills" and dried. Chipped or powdered cinnamon bark is one of the spices most widely used in home cookery. In food manufacturing, the bark serves primarily to flavor candy and baked goods, meat products, apple butter, and condiments. The extract is used to a lesser extent for the same purposes. The bark oil, distilled from scraps, enters mainly into soft drinks (especially of the "cola" type) and chewing gum, candy, and ice cream. Cinnamon leaf oil is strong, hot, and clovelike. It is most useful in chewing gum, condiments, and pickles, and for enhancing fruit and chocolate flavors in beverages, candy, and liqueurs. The tree requires a hot, humid climate. It may be propagated by cuttings, but is usually grown from seeds. In the Seychelles, many cinnamon trees have arisen from seeds dropped by birds.

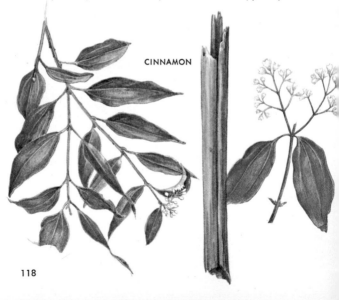

CINNAMON

CASSIA CINNAMON, or **CHINESE CINNAMON** (*Cinnamomum cassia*), is native to southeastern China and cultivated commercially in Kwangsi and Yunnan provinces, and in western Java and Tanzania. It is a tree (to 40 ft.) with thick, leathery leaves (to 6 in. long), glossy above, pale and slightly downy beneath. The bark is thicker and coarser than that of Ceylon cinnamon, is not fermented, but is scraped to remove the bitter outer layer, then dried until it turns brown and curls into tubes or "quills." Chinese cooks use it mainly as seasoning for pork and other meats. It is popular in western Asia, where it is used to flavor curries, confectionery, and beverages. In American food manufacturing, it is used in larger quantities than Ceylon cinnamon, primarily in baked goods (especially cinnamon buns and coffee cake). Cassia bark oil is important in chewing gum and also serves as flavoring for meat products, condiments, and candy. The fruits, picked unripe and dried, resemble cloves and are called **CASSIA BUDS.** Because of their strong flavor, they are esteemed in the Orient. In France, Germany, and the Soviet Union, they are favored for flavoring chocolate and pickles. In the United States, they are used solely in soft drinks. Leaves, leafstems, young twigs, and flower stalks are distilled for their essential oil. Crushed fresh leaves are steeped in water that the Chinese use for shampooing the hair.

CASSIA
CINNAMON

SAIGON CASSIA

INDONESIAN CASSIA

WILD CINNAMON

SAIGON CASSIA, or **SAIGON CINNAMON** (*Cinnamomum loureirii*), a tree (to 60 ft.), grows wild and is cultivated in Cambodia, Laos, and Vietnam. The bark of old Saigon cassia trunks is rich in essential oil, has a fine, sweet, pungent flavor, and is highly esteemed as a spice. Powdered Saigon cassia is preferred for cinnamon toast and for seasoning apple pie. The unripe fruits are dried and sold as cassia buds.

INDONESIAN, BATAVIA, or **MALAY, CASSIA** (*Cinnamomum burmanni*), native to Southeast Asia and cultivated in Java and Sumatra, is a shrub or tree (to 50 ft.) with glossy, leathery leaves (to 5 in. long) and strongly cinnamon-scented bark. The bark, taken from the trunk, is rolled into "quills" and exported to a limited extent as a spice. It is also pulverized and made into joss sticks.

WILD CINNAMON (*Cinnamomum iners*) is native to Southeast Asia, Indonesia, and the Philippines and often cultivated. It is a tree (to 60 ft.) with variable leaves (to 1 ft. long), dark and glossy above and with blue-gray, silky down on the underside. The flowers have an unpleasant odor but all other parts of the tree smell strongly of cinnamon. The bark is locally popular for seasoning foods, especially curries. The essential oil, distilled from the leaves, is used to flavor candy and sweetmeats. The wood is valued for paneling.

OLIVER'S BARK is derived from *Cinnamomum oliveri*, known as **BLACK, BRISBANE,** or **OLIVER'S, SASSAFRAS,** and native to Australia. The tree (to 80 or even 125 ft.) is ornamental, with glossy leaves (to 8 in. long) and thin, rough, fragrant bark and wood. The bark has a pungent, bitterish flavor resembling clove and sassafras combined, and is used locally for seasoning. Bushmen steep a small piece in their tea.

MASSOIA BARK is the product of the tree *Cinnamomum massoia*, native to New Guinea. The bark has a clove aroma and a pungent, bitterish but agreeable taste much like allspice. It was formerly exported to western Australia for distillation of the oil (which has a clove-nutmeg odor), for use in perfumery and medicine. Australians also made use of the bark for flavoring cakes and rolls. The oil has been recommended for use in confectionery, but it would require detoxification for it contains the harmful substance safrole, no longer permitted in flavorings.

INDIAN CASSIA (*Cinnamomum tamala*), of northern India and tropical Australia, is a tree (to 25 ft.) with especially aromatic leaves (to 6 in. long), called tejpat, which are gathered and dried in great quantities for local culinary flavoring. The bark is coarser than that of Ceylon cinnamon but is commonly used to adulterate it. The leaves of *C. obtusifolium* are also called tejpat in India and likewise used in cookery.

BLACK SASSAFRAS

Cinnamomum massoia

INDIAN CASSIA

121

BOIS DE ROSE

BRAZIL CLOVE

BOIS DE ROSE OIL, or ROSE-WOOD OIL, is obtained from *Aniba roseaodora*, indigenous to French Guiana, Surinam, Peru, and Brazil. It is an evergreen tree (to 100 ft.) with stiff leathery leaves (to 1 ft. long), downy-yellow on the underside, and woolly-brown terminal flower clusters. In 1875 a Frenchman first distilled from the bark and chipped wood the fragrant oil that is so esteemed in the perfume industry that the supply in French Guiana has been exhausted. Brazil is now the leading producer. In the food industry, the oil and its product, linalool, are used for flavoring baked goods, candy, ice cream, and chewing gum.

BRAZIL CLOVE, CLOVE BARK, or CAYENNE ROSEWOOD (*Dicypellium caryophyllatum*), native from the central Amazon region of Brazil to French Guiana, is a small tree, all parts of which are rich in clovelike aroma and flavor. The flower buds and the bark are popular seasonings in Brazilian cookery. Formerly the bark was exported to France and the oil distilled ("clove bark oil" or "clove cassia") for use in perfumery, but the oil is now in little demand.

122

MAY-CHANG (*Litsea cubeba*), which grows wild and is cultivated from northeastern India to South Vietnam, is a shrub or tree with deciduous leaves (to 4 in. long). All parts possess a pleasant lemon aroma. The delightfully scented flowers are used for flavoring tea and yield essential oil prized in perfume blending. Fragrant and peppery, the young fruits resemble, and are used as a substitute for, cubeb pepper. They are especially employed as seasoning to overcome the strong odor and taste of goat's meat and not-so-fresh fish. A small amount of the alkaloid laurotetanine in the bark, leaves, and fruit renders them slightly toxic.

CLOVE NUTMEG, or **MADAGAS-CAR CLOVE NUTMEG** (*Ravensara aromatica*), native to Madagascar and cultivated in Ceylon, is a tree (to 40 ft.) with leathery, clove-scented leaves and equally aromatic bark and fruits. The seed kernels, much like a blend of nutmeg and cloves in flavor, are popular as spice in Madagascar and have been exported to France. Leaves and bark are also used for seasoning. The bark is employed in making native rum.

MAY-CHANG

CLOVE NUTMEG

123

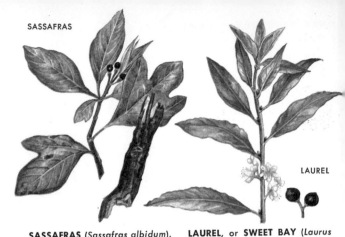

SASSAFRAS

LAUREL

SASSAFRAS (*Sassafras albidum*), native to the eastern United States, is a tree (60-80 ft. or over 100 ft.) with variably formed, aromatic leaves (to 5 in. long). Early settlers fermented the roots and branchlets with molasses to make beer. During the Civil War, sassafras tea made by boiling the roots in maple sap was very popular. Chips of the root bark are still sold today for making a tonic. The young leaves and stems, dried and pulverized and known as gumbo file, are used to thicken soup in Louisiana. The leaves are used commercially for the same purpose but must be freed of the toxic principle safrole. Formerly, safrole and sassafras oil were standard flavorings for root beer and other carbonated beverages but safrole is now banned. Sassafras bark extract (safrole-free) is employed in the manufacture of soft drinks, candy, ice cream, and bakery goods.

LAUREL, or **SWEET BAY** (*Laurus nobilis*), a native of the Mediterranean region, is cultivated commercially in southern Europe, the Canary Islands, the Near East, and China, and widely grown as a potted plant. It is a pyramidal evergreen tree (40-60 ft.) with stiff, spicy leaves (to 3½ in. long) and aromatic fruits (½-¾ in. long). In ancient Greece and Rome, wreaths for victorious warriors and other notables were made of the leaves. Dried leaves are used in Turkey and Italy to wrap licorice for export, and in China for packaging rice. In home cookery, sweet bay leaves give flavor to soup, fish chowder, roasts, stews, poultry, stuffings, gravies, sauces, salads, and vegetables. Industrially, they serve as seasoning for meat products, baked goods, and condiments. The leaf oil and extract are used mainly for flavoring condiments and the fruits in manufacturing soft drinks.

PAPAVERACEAE (Poppy Family)

POPPY SEED is a product of the **OPIUM POPPY** (*Papaver somniferum*), native to Turkey and cultivated mainly in Asia and Europe. It is an erect annual plant (2-6 ft.) with more or less lobed leaves (4-10 in. long) and flowers typically white but sometimes red, pink, purple, or bluish with purple eyes. The unripe seed capsule (1-3 in. wide) is scored daily to draw out the milky, narcotic sap (opium) which is the source of morphine, codeine, and other alkaloids. After the sap ceases to flow, the seed capsules ripen and are harvested. The seeds have been found in quantity at the site of Neolithic dwellings. They have a mildly spicy and oily flavor, and are much used whole as topping for breads, rolls, cakes, cookies, and confectionery. Crushed and sweetened seeds are popular fillings for pastries. In home cookery, the seeds are also used to flavor stews and vegetables. They are an ingredient of birdseed and also yield a bland oil used like olive oil.

OPIUM POPPY

CAPERBUSH

CAPPARIDACEAE (Caper Family)

CAPERS are the flower buds of the **CAPERBUSH** (*Capparis spinosa*), which occurs wild from Mediterranean Europe to northwestern India, and is cultivated mainly in Spain, France, and Italy. It is a spiny, trailing shrub (3-5 ft. high) with deciduous leaves (to 2 in. long), showy flowers, and slender, oval, long-stalked fruit. The flower buds have a sharp, burning taste. When young and tender, they are picked daily in early morning, and kept in a dark place for a few hours before being pickled in vinegar. Then known as capers, they are widely used as seasoning in rice dishes and cheese soufflés in Indonesia, and in salads, sauces for meats and seafood, and stuffings for baked fish in Europe and North America. Buds and immature fruits of related Asiatic species, including *C. decidua*, *C. zeylanica*, and *C. brevispina*, are similarly pickled and used.

BLACK
MUSTARD

WHITE
MUSTARD

CRUCIFERAE (Mustard Family)

MUSTARD SEED is obtained from several plants. The primary source is **BLACK MUSTARD** (*Brassica nigra*), originally from Eurasia and now almost universally cultivated. Black mustard is an annual (3-10 ft. or more), with somewhat hairy leaves and brilliant flowers. Its erect, smooth pods (⅜-¾ in. long) contain very small dark-brown seeds, yellow inside and exceedingly pungent. Next in importance as a source of mustard seed is **WHITE MUSTARD** (*B. hirta*, syn. *B. alba*), native to southern Europe and western Asia. It is an annual (2-4 ft. tall) with rough, hairy leaves (6-8 in. long) and paler flowers. Its bristly pods (1-1½ in. long) contain light-brown seeds, white inside, which are larger and less peppery than those of black mustard. Whole mustard seeds are used to season pickles, sausages, and sauerkraut. The ground seeds constitute mustard flour, or dry mustard, commonly used in curries in the Near East. Mixed with cold water or milk, dry mustard is a

INDIAN
MUSTARD

piquant seasoning for meats, poultry, seafood, cheese and egg dishes, and sauces. Commercially prepared mustard is generally made of a blend of black and white mustard seed, combined with vinegar as a preservative and turmeric for coloring. In the United States it is perhaps most extensively consumed on frankfurters and hamburgers. Mustard oil, distilled from the seeds of black mustard, is used to flavor pickles, canned goods, and condiments. Young leaves of white mustard are often cooked as greens. Another source of mustard seed, **INDIAN**, or **CHINESE, MUSTARD** (*B. juncea*), of India and China, is a variable, much-branched plant (2-4 ft. high) with nearly smooth leaves (6 in. to 1 ft. long), bright flowers, beaked pods (1½-2½ in. long), and dark reddish-brown, very pungent seeds which are often used whole to season meats and other foods. Mustard prepared from these seeds, called Sarepta, Russian, or Brown, mustard, is stronger than the ordinary kind. Young leaves are cooked and eaten as greens; supply vitamin B and carotene.

MORINGACEAE (Moringa Family)

HORSERADISH TREE (*Moringa oleifera*) is native to India and Arabia, and widely grown in tropical climates as a source of food and as an ornamental. It is a brittle tree (to 25 ft.) with ferny, compound leaves (to 2 ft. long), year-round masses of flowers, and a continuous crop of seedpods (to 1½ ft. long). The mustard-flavored mature leaves are cooked and added to various dishes as seasoning. Young leaves as well as flowers, immature pods, and seeds are cooked as vegetables. Mature seeds are roasted and eaten like nuts and also yield ben oil, valued for culinary and cosmetic uses. The root is acrid, resembling horseradish in aroma and flavor. Peeled roots of young trees are much used in India as a substitute for horseradish.

SLOE

HORSERADISH
TREE

ROSACEAE (Rose Family)

SLOE, or **BLACKTHORN** (*Prunus spinosa*), is native from Ireland and England to Iran and southwestern Siberia and sometimes cultivated. It is a thorny tree (to 15 ft.) with deciduous leaves (to 2½ in. long), fragrant white or pink flowers, and fruits (⅜-⅝ in. wide) with green flesh clinging to the stone. In the past, the leaves were used to adulterate tea. The fruits are acid and astringent (except for a sweet variety) and need mellowing by frost. They have been made into preserves and wine or added to other wines, and are used in Europe to flavor gin and liqueurs. Commercially, in the United States, the fruit extract is very important in flavoring alcoholic beverages, and is also used in soft drinks, ice cream, candy, and baked goods.

BITTER ALMOND (*Prunus communis* var. *amara*) is native to Asia Minor and Iran and cultivated primarily in Mediterranean countries. This tree (10-20 ft. high) has deciduous leaves (3-6 in. long) and white or red flowers. Its velvety fruit resembles a peach but is dry and splits open when ripe, revealing the smooth, pitted stone. The kernel is very bitter and highly poisonous, containing hydrocyanic acid. Bitter almond oil, distilled from the kernels (or more often from the kernels of apricots, peaches, plums, or cherries), is detoxified and used as flavoring for chewing gum, candy, baked goods, ice cream, puddings, Maraschino cherries, and soft drinks. It is especially useful in enhancing fruit flavors. Much of the so-called bitter almond in the trade is the less expensive refined synthetic benzaldehyde. **SWEET ALMOND** (var. *dulcis*) has an edible kernel that ranks as the leading tree "nut" in world trade. Sweet almond kernels are mixed with very small quantities of bitter almond kernels to make almond paste.

WILD BLACK CHERRY (*Prunus serotina*), also called **RUM**, or **WHISKY, CHERRY,** is native throughout the eastern and midwestern United States. It is a stately tree (40-60 or up to 100 ft.) with dark, bitter, aromatic bark, deciduous, glossy leaves (2-6 in. long), slender flower spikes, and bitter fruits. This is an important timber tree. The bark yields hydrocyanic acid

BITTER ALMOND

WILD BLACK CHERRY

SWEET CHERRY

and, when freed of this poison, is the source of an extract valued commercially as flavoring for alcoholic beverages, soft drinks, candy, syrups, and baked goods. The fruits have served to flavor brandy, but the pits are toxic. Extracts from the pits of the **SWEET CHERRY** (*P. avium*) and the **SOUR CHERRY** (*P. cerasus*) are used to flavor soft drinks and ice cream.

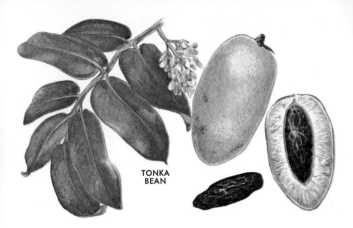

TONKA
BEAN

LEGUMINOSAE (Pea Family)

TONKA BEAN (*Coumarouna odorata*, syn. *Dipteryx odorata*) grows wild in northern South America and was long ago introduced into the Old World tropics. It is a stout tree (to 90 ft.) with compound leaves (4-6 in. long), very fragrant flowers, and a woody, aromatic fruit containing fibrous pulp and one seed. In the past, the seeds were used as a vanilla substitute in flavoring bakery products, candy, liqueurs, tobacco, and medicinal preparations. However, because they contain toxic coumarin, the seeds have been banned as a flavoring in the United States. Tonka beans are still used to flavor some foreign tobaccos and snuff. The extract and absolute are valued in perfume blending and in soaps. Several related species produce seeds used similarly.

BALSAM OF TOLU is obtained from the **BÁLSAMO** (*Myroxylum balsamum*) of Colombia, Venezuela, and Brazil. It is a spreading tree (30-65 ft. tall) with compound, glossy leaves, having up to 13 leaflets, and downy flower clusters. The seedpod (to 3 in. long) contains two round balsam pits, separated from the seeds. An aromatic, yellowish-brown gum exudes from V-shaped cuts made in the trunk of the tree and solidifies to a glasslike consistency. It has a cinnamon-vanilla odor and a spicy, cinnamonlike, slightly bitter taste. Commercially tolu balsam is used to some extent in baked goods and ice cream. The extract is more important for flavoring ice cream, candy, baked goods, soft drinks, and chewing gum. The essential oil is valued in perfumery.

BALSAM OF PERU is produced by *Myroxylum balsamum* var. *pereirae*, the **BÁLSAMO** of Central America, particularly El Salvador, one area of which the Spaniards called the balsam coast. The balsam was misnamed because it was sent to Europe on ships sailing from Peru. The tree is a handsome evergreen (50-100 ft. high), having 7-11 leaflets and only slightly hairy flower clusters. The winged seedpod (to 4 in. long) contains one seed at the thick end. In Guatemala, the seeds are put into aguardiente, just as a bitter almond may be put into a bottle of tequila in Mexico. Balsam collectors bruise the bark on four sides of the trunk and a few days later burn off these strips. Then the aromatic, dark-brown balsam flows out readily onto rags from which it is squeezed. It remains liquid and oily. It smells like cinnamon when fresh but acquires more of a vanilla fragrance with age. The flavor is hot, spicy, and bitter. The balsam serves as incense in Central American churches. As a flavoring, it is used mainly in chewing gum. Because of its bitterness, it plays a minor role in baked goods, candy, and other food products. It is greatly prized as an ingredient in rich, heavy Oriental-type perfumes and high-quality scents and soaps of many types.

BALSAM
OF PERU

FENUGREEK (*Trigonella foenum-graecum*) is native from Mediterranean Europe to northern India and extensively cultivated from Spain to China. It is an annual herb (1-2 ft. high) with compound leaves, attractive flowers, and seedpods (2-3 in. long) containing 10 to 20 brownish-yellow seeds. The entire plant has a strong, sweet-clover scent and is dried and mixed with stored grain as an insect repellent. The very bitter young leaves are cooked. When whole, the seeds smell of celery; crushing brings out an intensely spicy odor. The taste is peculiar—bitter, starchy, and oily. Women of Libya and Eritrea eat fenugreek seeds to gain weight, and the seeds are often added to cattle feed but must be deodorized to avoid tainting the milk. The seeds were used as spice by the ancient Egyptians, are common ingredients of curry powder and Oriental sauces, and valued also for seasoning and preserving butter. They are sometimes roasted as a substitute for coffee. As a commercial flavoring, fenugreek enjoys increasing use in condiments, candy, baked goods, ice cream, meat products, syrups, and soft drinks. The oleoresin is much used in making artificial maple syrup and also in puddings to create maple, vanilla, caramel, or butterscotch flavors, and enters into soft drinks. The extract serves somewhat the same purposes and is used in chewing gum. Fenugreek has had many medicinal uses and holds new promise as a source of diosgenin, from which sex hormones, oral contraceptives, and other pharmaceutical products may be derived.

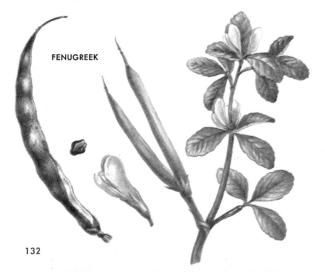

FENUGREEK

LICORICE

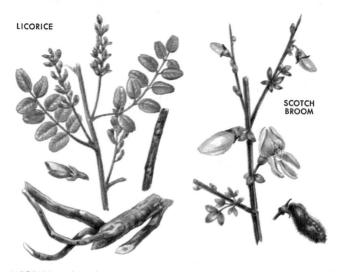

SCOTCH BROOM

LICORICE (*Glycyrrhiza glabra*) grows wild from Spain to northern India and is widely cultivated in Europe and Asia. It is a perennial subshrub (3-5 ft. high) with spreading roots, compound, sticky leaves, 4- to 6-inch flower spikes, and seedpods containing 3 or 4 kidney-shaped seeds. The roots contain glycyrrhizin, 50 times sweeter than sucrose. They are boiled to obtain the familiar solid extract from which licorice sticks are made. The roots, the powder, and extract are used in vast quantities in candy and chewing gum; to offset the bitterness in beer; and to flavor tobacco. Licorice also enters into some baked goods, ice cream, and soft drinks. The extract has a foaming action that makes it useful in fire extinguishers.

SCOTCH BROOM (*Sarothamnus scoparius*, syn. *Cytisus scoparius*), sometimes called **YELLOW BROOM**, grows wild in the British Isles, Europe, North Africa, and western Asia and is naturalized in Hawaii, Australia, and parts of the United States. It is a stiff, wiry shrub (to 8 ft.) with downy, compound leaves, attractive flowers, and hairy seedpods containing many glossy seeds. Young branchlets were formerly used alone or with hops to give beer a bitter flavor. The flower-buds have been pickled and eaten as a substitute for capers, especially in Germany, and the seeds roasted as mock coffee in France. Nevertheless, the plant —especially the young fruit— contains the toxic alkaloid sparteine and in quantity has proved fatal to grazing animals.

ERYTHROXYLACEAE (Coca Family)

COCA (*Erythroxylon coca*), native to the Peruvian Andes and cultivated intensely in Peru, Bolivia, and Colombia, also in Java and Ceylon, may be a shrub (2-5 ft.) or small tree (to 18 ft.). It has thin leaves (1½-2 in. long) which are chewed by millions of the poor in South America as a stimulant and to render themselves oblivious to their harsh environment and labors. Continuous use results in mental apathy and degeneration. The alkaloid, cocaine, derived from the leaves is a great blessing in medicine as an anesthetic, a curse if abused as an addictive drug. Coca leaf extract is decocainized and used extensively in the flavoring of "cola" beverages, candy, and ice cream.

COCA

ANGOSTURA

RUTACEAE (Rue Family)

ANGOSTURA (*Galipea officinalis*, syn. *G. cusparia*) is native to the Caroni region of Venezuela and northern Brazil. It is a slender tree (12-20 ft. tall) with glossy, compound leaves (6-10 in. long), tobacco-scented when crushed; and hairy, ill-smelling flowers. The fruit is normally a 5-celled capsule with 2 round black seeds in each cell. Formerly, the bark was much used medicinally, but it was found to be often adulterated with the poisonous bark of *Strychnos nux-vomica*. It has a spicy, pungent, bitter taste, stimulates the appetite, and was the original flavoring for Angostura Bitters, now made of bitter orange peel and other spices and herbs. True angostura extract is still used to flavor alcoholic beverages and soft drinks.

PRICKLY ASH, various species of *Zanthoxylum,* are common trees and shrubs in Asia and the Americas; more than a half-dozen eastern species are sources of seasonings popular in Oriental foods. Among the most important is the **SAN-SHO** (Z. *piperitum*), native to Korea, Japan, and northern China and cultivated in gardens in these countries and in Hawaii. It is a deciduous spiny shrub (4-5 ft. high) with tough, glossy, compound leaves (2-6 in. long) and rough, purplish-red fruit which splits open, showing a glossy black seed. The pungent bark, whole unripe fruits, and the separated seeds are ground up and commonly used as seasoning even though they are considered harmful if consumed habitually. The young, lemon-scented leaves are added to soup and boiled with meat and seafood as flavoring. They are also boiled with sugar and soy sauce to make a savory condiment. The **WINGED PRICKLY ASH** (Z. *alatum*) grows wild and is cultivated from central China through India and Southeast Asia, also in the Philippines and Japan. It is a spiny shrub or tree (to 15 ft.) with compound leaves, fuzzy flower spikes (2-6 in. long), and fruit composed of 3-4 lobes (sometimes aborted to 2), single-seeded and splitting open when ripe. All parts of the plant are highly aromatic and employed in folk medicine. The bark and fruits are insecticidal and used as fish poisons. The fruits have an appealing mint-and-pepper flavor. Under the name of **CHINESE PEPPER,** the seeds are much used in China and India as seasoning.

SAN-SHO

WINGED PRICKLY ASH

INDIAN PEPPER (*Zanthoxylum rhetsa*), also called **INDIAN IVY-RUE**, is native to the Coromandel coast of India, Malaya, Southeast Asia, and the Philippines. It is a deciduous tree (to 60 ft.) with stout thorns, compound leaves (6-20 in. long), and tiny flowers in branched clusters. The one-celled fruit (¼ in. wide), reddish-brown and crinkled when ripe, splits open, exposing the single seed. All parts of the tree are aromatic and contain coumarin derivatives and alkaloids. The corky bark has a lime-pepper flavor and is added to foods as seasoning, and is also cooked in syrup or honey and combined with ginger, mustard seed, and onions to make a sweet relish. In South Vietnam, Indian pepper leaves are used like hops in making rice beer. When green, the whole fruits taste like orange peel and are used as spice. The seeds taste like lemon, with a burning aftersensation; they are much used as a substitute for pepper. They are exported from Southeast Asia to China and Iran for spice and medicinal use.

CURRY LEAF TREE (*Murraya koenigii*) grows wild in Pakistan, India, Ceylon, and the Andaman Islands and is commonly cultivated throughout Southeast Asia and in Java. It is an ornamental shrub or tree (to 20 ft.) with compound leaves (to 15 in. long), downy on the underside, fragrant flowers, and edible, peppery, 2-seeded fruits. The leaves are highly aromatic, with a musky odor and flavor. They are staple ingredients in curries, chutneys, and stews, but are not used in commercial curry powders, which are made up of various combinations of spices.

INDIAN PEPPER

CURRY LEAF TREE

BUCHU, a relatively new spice in the food industry, is derived from two species of *Agathosma* (formerly *Barosma*), shrubs which grow wild and are cultivated in South Africa. The principal source is **ROUND-LEAF BUCHU** (*A. betulina*), a shrub (2½-3 ft.) with glossy leaves (½-¾ in. long) and pink flowers. **OVAL BUCHU** (*A. crenulata*, syn. *A. serratifolia*) is a bush (3-8 ft. tall) with purplish shoots, leaves ¾-1½ in. long, and white flowers having purple anthers. Where the plants are abundant, the air is filled with their powerful thymelike aroma. Dried buchu leaves are traded in the international pharmaceutical market. The leaves are also much used medicinally in South Africa, particularly as a diuretic. The remedy is commonly prepared as a brandy, sold in bars and taverns. In Tunisia, buchu brandy is produced not for medicinal purposes but as a base for highly popular cocktails. Buchu leaf extract is one of the ingredients of South African herbal wine. Hottentots powder their bodies with the pulverized leaves. The leaves are also steeped in vinegar, which is rubbed as a lotion on sprains and bruises. Buchu leaves are not known to be used locally as culinary seasoning. Bitter and astringent in taste, they yield an essential oil with a camphor-peppermint odor, which is used by American food manufacturers in candy, ice cream, baked goods, and condiments. However, buchu has so potent a flavor that it must be employed with extreme moderation.

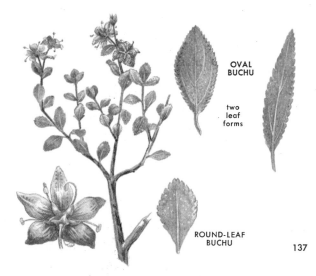

OVAL BUCHU

two leaf forms

ROUND-LEAF BUCHU

LEMON (*Citrus limon*) ranks among the leading flavor sources of the world. Lemon juice and grated lemon peel are indispensable in home cookery. A wedge or slice of lemon has become a standard accompaniment for iced tea. Lemon extract and oil are consumed in great quantities in candy, icings, baked goods, chewing gum, soft drinks, and many other food products. The **LIME** (*C. aurantifolia*) is known most widely for the concentrated bottled juice added to alcoholic drinks. The boiled juice is a common table sauce in Iran. Fresh lime juice is commonly used in the American tropics on fish and papaya. Frozen concentrated lime juice is widely marketed. Lime oil is used commercially mainly in chewing gum and candy, but also in the same classes of foods in which lemon flavor is employed. **SWEET ORANGE** (*C. sinensis*) deserves a place among spices, for the essential oil and extract from its peel are important flavorings for candy, baked goods, icings, ices, puddings, gelatin desserts, chewing gum, and soft drinks. Oil distilled from the peel of the **BITTER**, **SOUR**, or **SEVILLE**,

BITTER ORANGE

LEMON

FLORIDA LIME

SWEET ORANGE

WEST INDIAN LIME

ORANGE (*C. aurantium*) is used for the same purposes as that of the sweet orange, although to a lesser extent; combined with sweet orange oil, it is used to intensify the flavor of soft drinks. The peel of the Seville orange is prized in marmalade. In Iran the peel is used to flavor rice and vegetables. In Spain, the sour juice is squeezed on meats before or during cooking. The essential oil pressed from the peel of the unripe fruit was the original flavoring for the well-known Curacao liqueur, now largely flavored synthetically. Bitter orange flowers are distilled for perfume oils, and the left-over condensed water (Orange Flower Water) was formerly a popular culinary flavoring. Bigarade Oil, obtained from the bitter orange leaves and twigs, is important in perfumery and much used to enhance fruit flavors in the food industry. Essential oil expressed from the peel of the distinctive **BERGAMOT ORANGE** (*C. aurantium* var. *bergamia*) is of major importance in hard candy and tobacco flavoring; it has minor use in chewing gum, baked goods, and desserts. **GRAPEFRUIT OIL,** from the peel of *C. paradisi,* is valued primarily for enhancing the flavors of soft drinks and chewing gum, but is also used in candy, toppings, baked goods, ice cream, and gelatins. **UZU** (*C. junos*), with an exceedingly acid juice, is a common condiment in Japan.

GRAPEFRUIT

BERGAMOT ORANGE

UZU

SIMARUBACEAE (Quassia Family)

QUASSIA, or **BITTERWOOD** (*Quassia amara*), of northern South America and Trinidad, is a slender tree (to 25 ft.) with compound leaves (to 10 in. long), showy flower spikes, and fruit (every 3 years) composed of 4 or 5 black drupes. The bark and wood are very bittter. Water drunk from a quassia wood cup has been esteemed as a tonic. The wood is used to flavor beer. An extract is used in spirits, soft drinks, and baked goods. **JAMAICA QUASSIA** (*Picrasma excelsa*) is interchangeable.

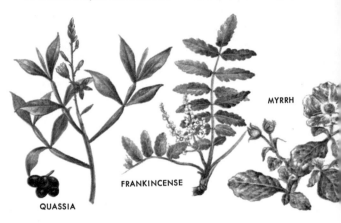

MYRRH

FRANKINCENSE

QUASSIA

BURSERACEAE (Torchwood Family)

FRANKINCENSE, or **OLIBANUM,** is obtained mainly from *Boswellia carteri* and *B. frereana*, small trees of western Asia and East Africa. The aromatic resin, at first a milky liquid, soon hardens into yellowish lumps called tears. It is used mostly as incense in churches. Locally it is chewed, and commercially it plays a small role in flavoring candy, baked goods, ice cream, and soft drinks.

MYRRH is obtained from several species of *Commiphora*, small thorny shrubs or trees with aromatic wood native to East Africa and western Asia. The fragrant, pungent gum-resin exudes from cuts made in the bark and hardens quickly. Of Biblical fame, it has much local use in incense and medicine. Commercially, it flavors soft drinks, soups, candy, and chewing gum and scents toiletries.

LINALOE (*Bursera aloexylon*), of southern Mexico, is a tree (15-20 ft.) with fragrant milky sap, compound leaves, and aromatic wood and berries. From the wood and fruits of the wild trees is distilled an essential oil of piquant, limelike, slightly bitter flavor. It is used to flavor candy, baked goods, ice cream, and soft drinks. A similar product is derived from *B. delpechiana*, also native to Mexico, and cultivated commercially in India.

LINALOE

MELIACEAE (Mahogany Family)

MOCK LIME (*Aglaia odorata*), wild and cultivated in China and Southeast Asia and grown in the East Indies, is an evergreen shrub or tree (to 50 ft.) with compound leaves (to 6 in. long) and fragrant flowers which are dried and added to tea. They are also used to perfume clothing and the body.

MOCK LIME

EUPHORBIACEAE (Spurge Family)

CASCARILLA, or **SWEETWOOD** (*Croton eluteria*, syn. *C. cascarilla*), grows wild in a few of the Bahama Islands and in Cuba. It is a spicily fragrant shrub or tree (7-15 ft. tall) with conspicuous leaves (1½-3 in. long), silver-velvety on the underside. The bark (sometimes called Eleuthera bark) is mildly bitter and aromatic, has pharmaceutical value, and has been employed to scent tobacco. The bark extract is used in soft drinks; the distilled oil in condiments, baked goods, candy, and ice cream.

CASCARILLA

ANACARDIACEAE (Mango Family)

SICILIAN, or **ELM-LEAVED, SUMAC** (*Rhus coriaria*), native throughout the Mediterranean region of Europe and central Asia and commonly cultivated, is a shrub (4-10 ft. high) with poisonous, milky sap, compound, downy leaves, erect, compact flower spikes (3-6 in. long), and woolly, sticky fruits of very acid flavor. The leaves have been famed for tanning light leathers since the early days of Rome. The fruit, especially popular with the Turks, Russians, and Iranis, is used to make a sour drink and a liquid seasoning. Dried and pulverized, it is a standard condiment at the table to give any food, particularly meat broths, an acid tang. The fruits are exported from Iran to India.

SICILIAN SUMAC

PEPPER TREE

PEPPER TREE, or **PERUVIAN PEPPER** (*Schinus molle*), native to Peru, is cultivated and naturalized in Mexico and Guatemala, long grown in California and the subtropics of the Old World. It is an erect tree (20-50 ft.) with compound leaves (6-9 in. long) and single-seeded fruits. The outer flesh is sweetish, the inner part pungent and bitter. Ingested in quantity, the fruit may cause intestinal inflammation and hemorrhoids. It is used to make intoxicating drinks in Peru, Chile, and Mexico. The dried, roasted berries are peppery and much used as a substitute for or adulterant of pepper in Latin America and in Greece, North Africa, and South Africa. A volatile oil distilled from the fruit is employed as a spice in baked goods and candy.

SAPINDACEAE (Soapberry Family)

GUARANÁ (*Paullinia cupana*), native from Colombia and southern Venezuela to Amazonian Brazil, is a climbing, woody shrub with coiled tendrils, compound leaves, inconspicuous flowers, and showy fruits. The black seeds (¾ in. long) contain both caffeine and tannin. Roasted, powdered guaraná seeds are pressed into paste which is dried and sold for making carbonated beverages and a stimulating "tea," often taken with milk and sugar. Some Indian tribes prepare a fermented, intoxicating drink. The sweetened paste is called Brazilian chocolate. It is used in the United States in soft drinks and candy, and is also used in flavorings for liqueurs.

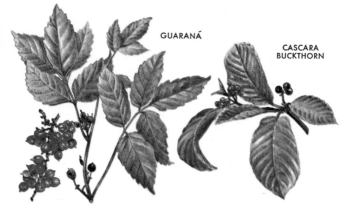

GUARANÁ

CASCARA BUCKTHORN

RHAMNACEAE (Buckthorn Family)

CASCARA BUCKTHORN (*Rhamnus purshiana*), native from British Columbia to California and Montana, and occasionally cultivated, is a dense shrub (4-12 ft.) in the southern part of its range, a tree (20-45 ft.) further north. It has handsome, glossy, deciduous leaves (2-6 in. long), tiny flowers, and smooth, usually 3-seeded, inedible fruits which become scarlet and then black. The bark ("cascara sagrada"), dried for at least a year, has been long used as a laxative. Although it is marketed commercially for pharmaceutical use, it is still harvested largely from wild trees as it was by the Indians and early settlers. It has a very bitter and peculiar taste. The extract, with the bitterness removed, is a common flavoring for soft drinks, baked goods, and ice cream.

BOMBACACEAE (Bombax Family)

MAHA, or MOLINILLO (*Quararibea funebris*), of southern Mexico, Guatemala, El Salvador, and Nicaragua, is a tree (to 65 ft.) with smooth leaves (5-16 in. long), fragrant flowers, and aromatic, fruit containing 1-4 seeds. The dried flowers (called *flor de cacao*) are peppery and mucilaginous. They are much used to flavor a cold drink made of chocolate and finely ground cornmeal consumed at festivals and weddings, and are also made into a tea to relieve coughs. Peeled stems of young trees, with whorled branches clipped short, are twirled to whip beverages to a foam. This tool is called a *molinillo*.

MAHA

MALVACEAE (Mallow Family)

AMBRETTE

AMBRETTE (*Abelmoschus moschatus*, syn. *Hibiscus abelmoschus*), believed native to India, is grown throughout the tropics. It is a bristly subshrub (2-3 ft.) with lobed leaves (4-6 in. long), showy flowers, and hairy seedpods (1-3 in. long). The unripe pods (called musk okra) are eaten cooked. Mature seeds are added to coffee in the Near East. Dried seeds or tinctures flavor liqueurs and tobacco. The costly distilled oil enhances baked goods, ice cream, candy, and soft drinks, but its major role is in perfumery. In Asia and Africa, the seeds are strung as necklaces or belts, or are powdered and rubbed on the body and hair as perfume and insect repellent.

STERCULIACEAE (Chocolate Family)

KOLA NUTS are the seed kernels of 6 or 7 species of the genus *Cola*, *C. nitida* and *C. acuminata* being the most valued commercially. Native to tropical West Africa, the trees (to 80 ft.) have glossy leaves (to 8 in.), small red or white flowers, and lumpy pods (to 6 in. wide) of 5-7 fingers. Each section holds 4-10 seeds individually encased in a tough, white, sweetish seedcoat which is removed after the seeds are soaked or sweated. The kernels (white, pink, or red) contain more caffeine than coffee, also a little theobromine. When fresh they are astringent because of their catechol and epicatechol content but drying renders these phenols insoluble.

Locally, the fresh kernels are preferred for chewing as stimulants. Kola nuts retard hunger and fatigue, greatly increasing the stamina of laborers, porters, dancers, explorers, military forces, and desert traders. In social ceremonies, they are tokens of hospitality, friendship, and congratulations. Bitter at first, the nuts create a sweet taste in the mouth and sweeten any food or drink taken immediately afterward. Kola nut extract, prepared from the dried (brown) kernels, is of the greatest importance in the manufacture of "cola" type carbonated drinks. It is also used as a flavoring in ice cream, candy, baked goods, and liqueurs.

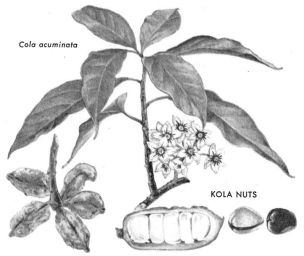

Cola acuminata

KOLA NUTS

CANELLACEAE (Canella Family)

CANELLA (*Canella winteriana*, syn. *C. alba*), also called **WILD**, or **WHITE**, **CINNAMON**, is native to extreme southern Florida and the Keys, the Bahama Islands, and the West Indies, and is cultivated in South Africa. The tree (shrubby or 30-50 ft. tall) has evergreen leaves (to 4 in. long), small red or purple flowers, and fruits which turn from green to red and finally black and contain small black seeds. Both the aromatic leaves and the bitterish, very pungent bark are used as condiments in the West Indies. The dried bark is exported to spice dealers and utilized in seasoning mixtures. It is added to smoking tobacco for its agreeable aroma when burned. The powdered bark was formerly prescribed as a stimulant and stomachic. However, the leaves and stems are now known to be toxic to domestic fowl.

CANELLA

LABDANUM

CISTACEAE (Rockrose Family)

LABDANUM, or **LADANUM** (*Cistus ladaniferus*), grows wild in Mediterranean Europe and Morocco and is grown in temperate gardens as an ornamental. It is a shrub (3-5 ft. high) with sticky leaves (2-4 in. long), downy-gray beneath, and attractive flowers. The plant exudes a fragrant, balsam-like resin, obtained by solvent extraction or by boiling the leaves and twigs. In the food industry, it is employed in baked goods, also soft drinks, ice cream, candy, and chewing gum. Widely used in perfumes and for scenting soaps and detergents, it is a valued substitute for ambergris. Similar resin is exuded by other species, including the **SHAGGY ROCKROSE** (*C. villosus creticus*) of Crete. There the resin is whipped from the bush onto leather thongs. In Cyprus, it is combed from the fleece of goats and sheep.

MYRTACEAE (Myrtle Family)

MYRTLE (*Myrtus communis*) occurs wild in southern Europe and western Asia and is widely cultivated as an ornamental. It is a compact shrub (to 15 ft.) with glossy, aromatic leaves (1-2 in. long) and fragrant flowers. The edible fruit, spicy and sweetish, contains several hard, white seeds. Dried fruits and flower-buds have been used as seasoning, and myrtle sprigs were formerly added to wine to increase its potency. Essential oil distilled from the leaves and twigs, and sometimes the flowers as well, is valued in perfume and is much used in food flavoring, especially with other spices in meat sauces and condiments. Myrtle was esteemed by the Greeks as a symbol of love, passion, and authority. To the Romans, it was a token of victory.

EUCALYPTUS OIL was formerly derived entirely from the Tasmanian **BLUE GUM** (*Eucalyptus globulus*) which, at present, yields about one fourth of the world supply (from plantations in Brazil and Spain). Today the greater part is produced in Australia from the **GULLY GUM** (*E. smithii*), together with the **YELLOW GUM** (*E. leucoxylon*) and the **BLUE MALLEE** (*E. polybractea*). Distilled from the fresh or dried leaves, the highly aromatic, pungent, bitterish oil is much used for scenting soaps, in perfumes and household deodorizing sprays, and for flavoring toothpaste and cough drops. It enters also into certain candies, baked goods, and ice cream. In some sensitive individuals, eucalyptus oil may cause allergic reactions.

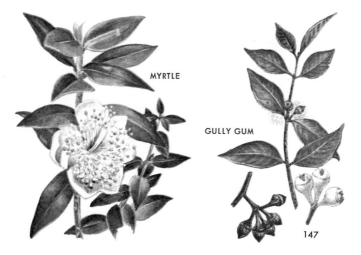

MYRTLE

GULLY GUM

ALLSPICE (*Pimenta dioica*, syn. *P. officinalis*), native to the West Indies and from northern South America to Mexico, is cultivated primarily in Jamaica. The tree (to 30 or 40 ft.) is erect, compact, and handsome, with delightfully aromatic evergreen leaves (to 5 in. long), abundant flowers in spring, and spicy, fragrant fruits, blackish-brown when ripe. Full-grown but still green fruits, dried in the sun, are the allspice of commerce, suggesting in aroma and flavor nutmeg, cloves, and cinnamon. Early Spanish explorers quickly adopted the spice, which the Mexicans added to chocolate, and it became one of the world's favorites. The berries and the essential oil are used to enhance fruit flavors and are important ingredients in baked goods, pickles, condiments, meats, chewing gum, soups, ice cream, confectionery, and soft drinks. Allspice leaves are used locally for culinary seasoning and are steeped for tea in Mexico and Cuba. The leaf oil serves to season meat products, condiments, baked goods, candy, and chewing gum. Both the fruit oil and leaf oil are employed in scenting men's toiletries.

WEST INDIAN BAY (*Pimenta racemosa*, syn. *P. acris*), also called **WILD CLOVE, WILD CINNAMON,** or **BAY-RUM TREE,** grows wild in the West Indies and northern South America and is cultivated to a small extent. It is an erect tree (to 40 ft.) with cylindrical crown, flaking bark, leathery evergreen leaves (to 6 in. long), and fragrant flowers. The fruits may be black or coated with fine gray hairs. Bay rum, formerly made by distilling the strongly aromatic leaves in rum, was long popular as a hairdressing and after-shave lotion. Today, bay leaf oil is obtained by steam- or water-distillation and utilized in perfume blends as well as in men's toiletries. In food manufacturing, the leaf oil, oleoresin, and extract are variously used to flavor soups, meats, and condiments. Trees in plantations are kept conveniently low by topping during the harvesting of the leaves.

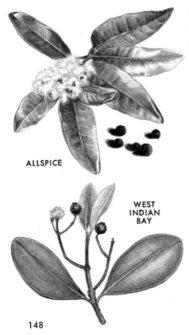

ALLSPICE

WEST INDIAN BAY

UMBELLIFERAE (Carrot Family)

ASAFETIDA is a gum-resin derived from *Ferula asafoetida*, *F. narthex*, and related species which grow wild in Central Asia. The plants, sometimes called **GIANT FENNEL**, are perennials (5-8 ft. tall) with downy foliage (basal leaves 1-2 ft. long), large, spindle-shaped roots, and an unpleasant odor. In spring, when the plant is about to bloom, it is cut off together with the top of the root. Milky resin exudes from the cut surface, is scraped off, and more exudes as successive slices of root are removed over a period of 3 months. The gummy resin is formed into "tears," lumps, or paste. It has a bitter, acrid taste and smells of garlic, but is much used in Asia for seasoning sauces, pickles, and curries. It is a standard ingredient in Worcestershire sauce and is widely employed in spice blends and condiments. The extract is used in soups and even ice cream. Asafetida leaves are locally cooked as greens.

ASAFETIDA

GALBANUM

GALBANUM is a gum-resin obtained primarily from *Ferula galbaniflua* in Iran. The plant is a stout perennial (to 4 ft. in height) with grayish, hairy leaves. The resin may be collected where it exudes from the base of the leafstalks and the main stem or from the exposed tissue of the living root, or by cutting off the plant and removing slices of the root from time to time to promote resin flow. The marketed lumps are orange-yellow or brownish outside, yellowish or bluish-green inside, with a bitter taste and a celery-like odor. Galbanum is used mainly for medicinal purposes, but the resin and its essential oil are sometimes employed in perfumery and as flavoring in condiments and a few other commercial food products. Plucking the leaves prepares the plant for resin production.

149

CUMIN (*Cuminum cyminum*), originally from the Upper Nile region and of ancient cultivation in North Africa, Arabia, Mediterranean Europe, India, and China, is today increasingly grown from Central Asia to Japan. It is an annual herb (to 1 ft. high) with dark-green leaves divided into slender segments (to 3 in. long) and tiny white or reddish flowers. The fruit, hairy, 7-ribbed, and popularly called cumin seed, has a strong "bedbug" odor disliked by many people, and a flavor somewhat like caraway but very "hot" and bitter. It is a popular flavoring for certain European breads and cheeses, and is also much used in highly seasoned foods such as Spanish and Mexican dishes, chutneys, and curries. The ground spice is a standard ingredient of commercial curry powder. In food manufacturing, cumin is most important in flavoring baked goods, meats, and condiments. The oil distilled from it enters mainly into condiments, sausages, meat sauces, pickles, cheeses, and liqueurs. It is employed sparingly in Oriental-type perfumes.

CUMIN

PIPSISSEWA

PYROLACEAE (Shinleaf Family)

PIPSISSEWA (*Chimaphila umbellata*), also called **PRINCE'S PINE**, is Eurasian, but the variety *cisatlantica* is wild in North America from Quebec to Indiana; variety *occidentalis* continues west to California, and variety *mexicana* grows in southern Mexico. It is a perennial subshrub (to 1 ft. high) with creeping rootstock and spreading stems, glossy leaves (1-2 in. long), and white or lavender-pink, fragrant flowers. The leaves stay green all winter, are aromatic when crushed, and have a refreshing, bitter, astringent, yet sweetish flavor. Among the American Indians, the plant infusion was a popular remedy; modern research has confirmed its antibiotic activity. Pipsissewa was formerly much used in homemade root beer. Today the leaf extract is a flavoring for candy and soft drinks.

STYRACACEAE (Storax Family)

STORAX, or AMERICAN STYRAX, is a gummy resin derived from the **SWEET GUM** (*Liquidambar styraciflua*), native to the eastern and southern United States, southern Mexico, and Central America. This giant tree (to 100 ft. high with trunk to 4 ft. thick) has deciduous leaves (to 8 in. long), vividly and variously hued in the fall. Male flowers are borne in erect spikes, female in pendant, round clusters. The fruit is a woody, spiny ball. Exuding naturally or from incisions, the resin solidifies on exposure to air; it is prized locally for medicinal uses and is chewed to sweeten the breath or clean the teeth. In the past, it was burned for incense and valued for flavoring tobacco. It has a balsam odor and a bitter, hot, cinnamon flavor. **ASIAN STYRAX** is a similar substance obtained from *L. orientalis* in Asia Minor. The resin of both species is important in the perfume industry and is used commercially in chewing gum, baked goods, and candy.

SWEET
GUM

BENZOIN

BENZOIN is a resin produced by several species of *Styrax*, especially *S. benzoin* (Sumatra benzoin), wild and cultivated in Sumatra, Java, and Malaya, and *S. tonkinensis* (Siam benzoin), native to Laos and North Vietnam. *S. benzoin* is a tree (30-100 ft. tall) with entire or finely toothed leaves, downy-white on the underside, and fragrant flowers. The resin is collected from gashes in the trunk and hardens on exposure. Siam benzoin (so named because of its export route) is yellow, orange, or pale brown, vanilla-scented, slightly acrid and bitter, and the most costly. Sumatra benzoin is whitish-gray or brown and has a cinnamon odor and more acrid taste. Both resins are extensively employed in incense, perfume, and scents for soap, as well as in pharmaceutical products. As flavoring, both are utilized in chewing gum, baked goods, puddings, soft drinks, and candy. Benzoin was formerly much used to flavor chocolate.

OLEACEAE (Olive Family)

JASMINE, or **POET'S JASMINE** (*Jasminum officinale*), is native from Iran to China and widely cultivated as an ornamental and for spice in Europe and North Africa. It is a shrub with long, climbing stems, compound leaves with 5-7 leaflets (½-2½ in. long), and highly fragrant flowers which, in variety *grandiflorum* (Spanish jasmine) are 1½ in. wide. The essential oil, esteemed as scent since ancient times, is one of the most treasured modern perfumes. As flavoring, the oil and extract impart a bittersweet, floral tone to baked goods, ice cream, candy, chewing gum, and Maraschino cherries. In China, the dried flowers of **ARABIAN JASMINE** (*J. sambac*) scent tea.

JASMINE

LABIATAE (Mint Family)

PATCHOULI

PATCHOULI (*Pogostemon cablin*) is native to the East Indies; cultivated mainly in the Philippines, Indonesia, and the Seychelles. It is a subshrub (to 3½ ft.) with aromatic, hairy leaves (2-4½ in. long) and mauve flowers in 1- to 3-in. spikes. Essential oil distilled from the dried, cured leaves has a rich, sweet, mint-sandalwood fragrance and is in great demand for perfume. As a flavoring it is used in chewing gum and for breath-sweetening lozenges and, to a lesser extent, in baked goods and candy. An inferior oil, **JAVA PATCHOULI,** or **DILEM,** is derived from *P. heyneanus* of India and Malaya.

HYDROPHYLLACEAE (Water-leaf Family)

YERBA SANTA (*Eriodictyon californicum*, syn. *E. glutinosum*) occurs wild from southern Oregon to Tulare County, California. It is a shrub (2-8 ft. tall) with thick, evergreen leaves (2-5 in. long), dark and glossy above and gray-felty beneath. The flowers may be dark or light violet or white. A yellowish, varnish-like resin makes the upper surface of the leaves and the stems sticky to the touch. The aromatic leaves have a sweetish, acrid flavor, reminiscent of balsam. They have been chewed to relieve thirst and used as a tobacco substitute and in home remedies, including a popular tonic "tea." The leaf extract is a commercial flavoring in pharmaceutical products as well as in baked goods, candy, ice cream, and soft drinks. The more southerly species, *E. crassifolium* and *E. trichocalyx*, have the same common name and local uses. Since all are rich in phenolics, they may prove unwholesome in quantity.

YERBA SANTA

SANDALWOOD

SANTALACEAE (Sandalwood Family)

SANDALWOOD (*Santalum album*), native to the East Indies and naturalized and cultivated in India, is a graceful tree (to 15 ft.), its roots partly parasitic on those of other plants. It has evergreen leaves (1½-2½ in. long), greenish to maroon flowers, and fleshy fruits containing hard, rough seeds. The fragrant white or yellowish heartwood, cherished by Orientals for 4,000 years, was first noticed by Europeans in the early 1800's. It quickly became a nearly priceless object of trade and conquest, with many wild stands being ravished. While the Chinese esteemed sandalwood for incense and cabinetry, and in India the pulverized wood was a treasured body powder, Europeans valued sandalwood for medicinal use and perfumery. The essential oil is still important in modern fragrances. As a flavoring, it is used in chewing gum, bakery products, ice cream, and candy, including breath-sweeteners.

153

SOLANACEAE (Nightshade Family)

RED PEPPER is derived from several species of *Capsicum*, mainly *C. annuum*, *C. frutescens*, and *C. chinense*, believed native to Central America and South America. These perennial subshrubs (to 8 ft.) are grown in temperate climates as annuals. The leaves are variable (1-5 in. long), the flowers white or purple-tinted, and the fruits may turn from green to yellow, then purple, and finally bright red. There are several races and cultivars. Variety *grossum* bears the sweet or bell pepper of mild flavor used unripe as a vegetable and ripe as paprika, fresh, pickled, or dried and pulverized as a spice. In the pungent races, the fruits may be round or conical, or elongated and pointed, sometimes curved. They range from ½ in. to 1 ft. in length. Variety *longum* produces cayenne and chili peppers. Hot peppers, green or ripe, whole, dried, or pickled, are in demand as condiments, or variously crushed or ground for seasoning. They are indispensable to Mexican, Indonesian, and Italian dishes, and piquant sauces such as Tabasco. Large amounts are utilized in sausages and other meat products and barbecue-flavored potato chips and crackers. Handling raw hot peppers irritates the skin. Contact with the eyes causes severe inflammation.

RED PEPPER

RUBIACEAE (Coffee Family)

CINCHONA BARK is obtained primarily from the **RED CINCHONA** (*Cinchona succirubra*) and **YELLOW CINCHONA** (*C. calisaya* and its variety *ledgeriana*), or from hybrids between these and other species. The first is a native of Ecuador; the second, of Bolivia and Peru. Both have been most intensively cultivated in Indonesia but many New World plantations have been established since 1940. They are stout trees (to 80 ft. high) with evergreen, downy leaves (6 in.-1 ft. long), sometimes red beneath, and rose-pink or ivory flowers. The bitter and astringent bark is famed as the source of quinine. In addition to this important pharmaceutical use, cinchona bark and extract are employed in bitters, alcoholic beverages, soft drinks, condiments, baked goods, and ice cream.

RED CINCHONA

YELLOW CINCHONA

INDEX

Note: sp. = species

158

**Photo credits: p. 5, J. F. Morton; p. 7, Brooklyn
Botanic Garden; p. 9, University of Miami Library.**

Front cover illustration: Borage (left) and *Myristica fragrans*, source
of nutmeg and mace (right). **Back cover illustration:** Pepper.